LYOTARD

For Claire

LYOTARD

Towards a Postmodern Philosophy

James Williams

Polity Press

First published in 1998 by Polity Press
in association with Blackwell Publishers Ltd.

Editorial office:
Polity Press
65 Bridge Street
Cambridge CB2 1UR, UK

Marketing and production:
Blackwell Publishers Ltd
108 Cowley Road
Oxford OX4 1JF, UK

Published in the USA by:
Blackwell Publishers Inc.
Commerce Place
350 Main Street
Malden, MA 02148, USA

A catalogue record for this book is available from the British Library.

Library of Congress Cataloging-in-Publication Data
Williams, James.
    Lyotard : towards a postmodern philosophy / James Williams.
        p.   cm.
    Includes bibliographical references and index.
    ISBN 0-7456-1099-4 (alk. paper). — ISBN 0-7456-1100-1 (pbk. :
alk. paper)
    1. Lyotard, Jean François.   I. Title.
B2430.L964W55   1998
194—dc21   98-23964
                                                                      CIP

Typeset in 10½ on 12 pt Palatino
by Ace Filmsetting Ltd, Frome, Somerset
Printed in Great Britain by T J International, Padstow, Cornwall

This book is printed on acid-free paper.

Key Contemporary Thinkers

Published

Jeremy Ahearne, *Michel de Certeau: Interpretation and its Other*
Peter Burke, *The French Historical Revolution: The Annales School 1929–1989*
Colin Davis, *Levinas: An Introduction*
Simon Evnine, *Donald Davidson*
Edward Fullbrook and Kate Fullbrook, *Simone de Beauvoir: A Critical Introduction*
Andrew Gamble, *Hayek: The Iron Cage of Liberty*
Phillip Hansen, *Hannah Arendt: Politics, History and Citizenship*
Sean Homer, *Frederic Jameson: Marxism, Hermeneutics, Postmodernism*
Christopher Hookway, *Quine: Language, Experience and Reality*
Simon Jarvis, *Adorno: A Critical Introduction*
Douglas Kellner, *Jean Baudrillard: From Marxism to Post-Modernism and Beyond*
Chandran Kukathas and Phillip Pettit, *Rawls: A Theory of Justice and its Critics*
Lois McNay, *Foucault: A Critical Introduction*
Philip Manning, *Erving Goffman and Modern Sociology*
Michael Moriarty, *Roland Barthes*
William Outhwaite, *Habermas: A Critical Introduction*
John Preston, *Feyerabend: Philosophy, Science and Society*
Susan Sellers, *Hélène Cixous: Authorship, Autobiography and Love*
David Silverman, *Harvey Sacks: Social Science and Conversation Analysis*
Geoffrey Stokes, *Popper: Philosophy, Politics and Scientific Method*
Georgia Warnke, *Gadamer: Hermeneutics, Tradition and Reason*
James Williams, *Lyotard: Towards a Postmodern Philosophy*
Jonathan Wolff, *Robert Nozick: Property, Justice and the Minimal State*

Forthcoming

Alison Ainley, *Irigaray*
Maria Baghramian, *Hilary Putnam*
Sara Beardsworth, *Kristeva*
Michael Caesar, *Umberto Eco*
James Carey, *Innis and McLuhan*
Thomas D'Andrea, *Alasdair MacIntyre*
Eric Dunning, *Norbert Elias*
Jocelyn Dunphy, *Paul Ricoeur*
Graeme Gilloch, *Walter Benjamin*
Christina Howells, *Derrida: Deconstruction from Phenomenology to Ethics*
Paul Kelly, *Ronald Dworkin*
Valerie Kennedy, *Edward Said*
Carl Levy, *Antonio Gramsci*
Harold Noonan, *Frege*
Wes Sharrock and Rupert Read, *Kuhn*
Nick Smith, *Charles Taylor*
Nicholas Walker, *Heidegger*

Contents

Acknowledgements

I am grateful to the University of Dundee Research Initiative Fund for a grant towards my research on Jean-François Lyotard and French philosophy.

The author and publishers are grateful for permission to quote from the following works by Jean-François Lyotard: *The Differend: Phrases in Dispute*, trans. George Van Den Abeele, Manchester University Press and University of Minnesota Press, 1988, by kind permission of the publishers; *Libidinal Economy*, trans. Iain Hamilton Grant, Athlone Press and Indiana University Press, 1993, by kind permission of the publishers.

1

Introduction: Rethinking the Political

Jean-François Lyotard's work is indispensable to any reflection on the most difficult problems of late twentieth-century society and culture. In his definition of the postmodern condition, he gives us an overview of these problems and one of the most important theories to draw them together. Lyotard reflects on the relation between the social fragmentation of contemporary societies and the global interconnection of markets and media. In fact, the concern with this relation, between radical differences and structures that attempt to bridge them, connects his account of the postmodern to his work as a whole. He tries to structure and decide upon the opposition of positive and negative reactions to fragmentation and globalization. Should we rejoice in differences drawn out of the end of unifying forces such as religion, nationhood, universal ideals? Or should we lament the passing of systems that legislate against conflict and difference in the name of greater progress and community? What are the political implications of fragmentation? How can we act with justice if there are no universal moral or legal norms?

A first response to these questions extends Lyotard's influence to the arts. According to his philosophy, if we are to testify to difference and to fragmentation, then we must do so in art and literature. He is also, therefore, an all-important theorist of and apologist for avant-garde arts. His contribution there is as important as his political and social theory. In his work, we find new and influential ways of thinking about the avant-garde and the experience of art. The political and philosophical roles of aesthetic experiences and creativity are thought anew and in a manner consistent with the latest representations of society, language and individuals. This explains his ubiquity in works on the postmodern, whether at the level of politics, sociology, philosophy, literature or art. Where all these spheres are considered in unison, in terms of general theories of postmodernity, he is invariably one of the main protagonists. This does not mean that he is taken as correct. The contrary is more often the case: Lyotard is the main representative of a strain of divisive postmodern thought that many have sought to prove wrong or to decry. This is because he champions difference and division against reconciliation. But the role of villain does not detract from his importance. It is impossible to understand the resurgence of arguments on modern values without referring to his attack on them.

The great frequency of references to Lyotard's work across a wide range of topics can also be explained by the pivotal role played by his writing in terms of schools of thought and influential debates. This role is best surveyed through an analysis of the main stages of his career, from his earliest postwar essays to his latest works. His first consistent set of essays (1956–63), collected in *La Guerre des Algériens* (1989) and translated in *Political Writings* (1993), brings together Marxist theory and a critical concern with a development of Marx in the context of the struggle for Algerian independence. These essays link him to Marxism, but also to theories on the development of Marxism by, for instance, Cornelius Castoriadis and Jean Baudrillard. His next main publication, *Discours, figure* (1971), connects poststructuralism, Marx and Freud in a critique of phenomenology through a study of art. In *Économie libidinale* (1974), Lyotard's work rejoins the post-1968 rebellion against theory and turns towards materialist enactments of desire. This book connects him to Deleuze and Guattari and to the contemporary attempt to think beyond Marx and Freud.

Later, Lyotard drifts away from this extreme materialism and his work takes a turn towards a combination of aesthetics, social critique and analytic philosophy of language, in the context of the postmodern. This work is announced in *La Condition postmoderne* (1979), but the key book is *Le Différend* (1983). He claims that this is his most philosophical work. It has become an important book for questions of justice and political action within the postmodern condition. Lately, Lyotard has contributed to debates on postmodern ethics and aesthetics in the collections *L'Inhumain* (1988) and *Moralités postmodernes* (1993). Lyotard's pivotal role does not only reflect movements. He has entered into important debates with many of the most influential thinkers of his generation: Derrida, Levinas,

Nancy, Lacoue-Labarthe, Habermas (by proxy), Rorty, Deleuze and Guattari. These debates and his original work on the postmodern also involve interpretations of key figures from the history of philosophy, notably Marx, Freud, Kant and Wittgenstein. Put together, his contribution to important debates, his position within key movements and his influential definition of the postmodern explain why future developments across many subjects will continue to depend on reactions to his work. Our contemporary desire to think 'after' the postmodern must refer back to Lyotard, not only for historical accuracy in terms of theory, but in terms of lessons to be drawn from his efforts to think 'with' the postmodern condition.

Thus, in a century when specialization has become the norm, the work of Jean-François Lyotard stands out for its range and variety. Few contemporary thinkers have had his ability and determination to cover and contribute to topics and subjects as disparate as art and aesthetics, politics and active political engagement, the philosophy of language, psychoanalysis, the interpretation of texts from the history of philosophy, literary criticism and critical analysis, and social critique. This richness is as rare as it is difficult to maintain, for the price of the division of his efforts could be that depth is achieved nowhere. This book seeks to show that, with Lyotard, philosophical range is accompanied by profundity, and what appears at first sight to be mere variety is in fact a variation and a deepening of thought across a wide area. Here thought reacts against the pressures which force philosophy towards specialization and away from an engagement with the complex connections which bring together the multiple aspects of modern life and societies.

My account of Lyotard's philosophy depends on the isolation of a central concern that runs through most, if not all, of his work: a rethinking of the political. Here 'political' stands for all forms of action linked to change, or resistance to change, in our societies. Politics is not limited to political parties or institutions. In fact, these may be seen to be far removed from political action – for example, when financial markets are seen to control the future of nations. Yet a series of familiar political and philosophical positions can be used to justify acts within this broad definition of the political. In line with this broad view of the political, Lyotard develops a wide-ranging philosophy that allows him to discard established positions with regard to political action, values and institutions. These are then replaced by new forms of action in tune with a new way of thinking about how acts can bring about just or valuable outcomes. For example, his later philosophy runs against any appeal to universal rights as the basis for action. Instead, the just act involves a recognition of radical differences between individuals, cultures and systems. These differences cannot be bridged by an appeal to the universality of rights. Similarly, in the case of the dominance of financial markets as agents of change, Lyotard's philosophy rejects the argument that claims that the greatest performance and hence the greatest well-being can be achieved in capitalist systems. Instead, he draws our attention to the necessary injustice of systems dependent on a criterion of performance that cannot be sensitive to radically different ways of living.

This disruptive and original way of thinking about political action depends on a teasing out of a set of recurring figures typical of Lyotard's work: the idea of the limit, the event, absolute difference and the avant-garde. The central concern and the recurring figures are brought together in his dissatisfaction with established or traditional ways of thinking about the political dimension in art, philosophy and linguistics. Thus the figures provide a new frame of reference for thinking the political, for example in Lyotard's turn away from totalization and towards fragmentation, which can be traced back to his awareness of the importance of limits and absolute difference. Thus, at the same time as political thinking undergoes a radical change through a reflection on different topics, the thought of the political in those topics is rebased and reinvigorated:

> What I have to tell you is driven by a work that is neither linguistic, nor semiological, not even philosophical, but rather *political*. This, in a sense of political that is not institutional (parliament, elections, political parties . . .), nor Marxist, a sense too close to the one already dismissed – political in a sense that is not determined yet and that will always, must always, remain to be determined. (Lyotard 1973: 127)

The stress on a sense of the political which involves a duty to desist from final definitions and judgements, and which defeats the will to determine the political with any such finality, is characteristic of Lyotard's approach to the political. For example, Bill Readings gives an illuminating account of this understanding of the political in the context of the modern–postmodern opposition (1993: xiii). Lyotard's work reflects a suspicion of knowledge as a basis for action. There will always be limits to such knowledge and the task of philosophy can be seen as revealing them in and through art and language.

Lyotard's most famous book, *The Postmodern Condition*, attempts to reflect on the political aspects of modern science and knowledge in terms of their claims to validity. Where claims to truth in science would appear to be above the raw competition more readily associated with politics, he shows that they involve conflicts that can only be understood as power struggles at the boundaries of different social practices. Thus, although different social practices (science and art, for example) involve quite legitimate rules when they operate within their proper spheres, these rules fail at their limits. There are valid tests of the validity of a scientific hypothesis; however, when this hypothesis is used in a social application then it enters into competition with other rules from other practices. For instance, it is possible and legitimate for medicine to determine the best form of treatment for a given illness, but that 'best' treatment becomes involved in a further struggle when financial and ethical considerations come into play. There may be best treatments from many different points of view: the most effective, the most economical, one that saves more valuable lives (the young, for instance). Lyotard's work in *The Postmodern Condition* is a rethinking of the political because it insists on the political element that enters into any discussion once claims from different spheres come into contact with one another.

This also explains how the book fits into Lyotard's work as a whole. It is a particular instance of his thought on the way specific philosophical problems become part of practical political struggles. In *The Postmodern Condition*, the incommensurability of language games (that is, the way rules from different spheres are inconsistent) throws all action at the boundaries between spheres into a power struggle. Lyotard's philosophy is characterized as the effort to understand and guide this struggle across a wide range of topics and issues.

In no way, though, does my decision to focus on a central concern imply a lack of interest in Lyotard's analysis of society, his theories of language, or in his studies of law and morality. On the contrary, these are the most interesting and influential facets of his philosophy, alongside his work on aesthetics and modern art. It is more that these facets are best understood when they are seen as leading to a rethinking of the effort to bring about change in society through a political act. Though this does not imply that Lyotard has always wanted to act 'for society', or even less 'for a new society'. He has advocated utterly rebellious acts that break the organization of society and turn to individual or group desires and interests. The consideration of the political act allows us to make sense of the models of society found in his works, but that consideration can only be felt with full force in those models. The rethinking of the political also allows us to appreciate Lyotard's understanding of the fabric of the world, his rules for moral practice or his attacks on such rules, his aesthetics, his theory of language and his study of avant-garde art. Again, these aspects of Lyotard's philosophy can be studied alone, but never to the same effect as when an eye is kept on the evaluation and critique of the political acts they entail. For example, it will be shown that the sense of 'avant-garde' is fully political in art, but also that the sense of 'political' is revolutionized by avant-garde art. The deepest sense of the political comes with the avant-garde, as it disturbs established knowledge and laws, and turns our attention to the constant possibility of further disturbances.

Lyotard's most extended study of art *Discours, figure*, his well-known articles on the figure, the libidinal and the sublime in art, as well as his studies of individual artists like Duchamp, show this application of philosophy to art in terms of revolutionary acts. Here, the shock value and innovation of the work of art take on a political significance as acts that disturb an established status quo and force us to think anew. Artists can show the limits and flaws of set ways of thinking and acting. They can return us to more fundamental sensations that have become hidden under elaborate forms of thought. Lyotard's influence among artists and aestheticians can be explained by this philosophical engagement with the work of art as a motivator of revolutionary action and thought.

The political act or, more accurately, the planning of such an act sets a series of awkward and inhibiting questions in motion: questions as to the best course of action to take, as to the most just course of action, as to why any action is necessary or even possible, questions as to where to act and as to what is sought as an end to the action. All are pushed to the fore as soon as we plan anything. Experience, often painful, teaches us to be wary of acts. There is a deep fount of wisdom on the dangers and pitfalls of idealist action, perhaps expressed most famously by Robert Burns in 'To a mouse' (1990: 72):

> The best-laid schemes o' Mice an' Men
> Gang aft agley,
> An' lea'e us nought but grief an' pain,
> For promis'd joy!

However, the counterbalance to this wisdom born of experience is equally persuasive: what is the point of thought and feeling if it does not lead to action? Aristotle shows us the real sadness of Burns's lesson: 'so those who act win, and rightly win, the noble and good things in life' (Aristotle 1925: s. 1099 a.). The role of a philosophy of action, of a philosophy aimed at a political commitment within society, is to answer the questions raised at the outset of action. It is to resolve the conflict of two forms of wisdom, wisdom born of painful experience and wisdom aware of the futility of an action-free existence – scepticism against commitment and commitment against scepticism. The questions arising at the outset of an action are the expression of that scepticism, but also, the fact that these questions have been raised at all is testament to a commitment, a will towards action in the world. Lyotard thinks on the cusp of this commitment and of the questions put forward by the sceptic, the voice of experience. In his early works on Algeria and in his works around the postmodern, he attempts to resolve the tension between political optimism and scepticism. His libidinal philosophy is more of an effort to ignore their debilitating effects. This depends on the argument that the effects come to bear only on certain forms of political action, in particular those that depend on negative critique or on utopian ideals.

To understand Lyotard in this way is to respond to his own political commitment, again in the widest sense of a reflection on the acts designed to change society or to change specific elements in society, rather than in the narrow sense of a deliberation on the government of society. This commitment can be found in his earliest works, for example in an essay for Jean-Paul Sartre's *Temps Modernes*, 'Nés en 1925', written when Lyotard was twenty-three. (In 1948 the French review *Temps Modernes* commissioned three students born in 1925 to record their observation on life after the war; Lyotard was one of them.) The essay strives for an appropriate response to the horror of the Second World War and to the implication of prewar politics and ethics in the horror (a preoccupation that was to stay with Lyotard for the rest of his life, recurring in the name Auschwitz):

> We will come out of war, the Twentieth Century's most concrete product, with a monstrous poverty of thought and morals. We are twenty years old when the camps disgorge that which they have had neither the time nor the appetite to digest. Those hollow faces plague our thinking: in the camps, Europe has assassinated its liberalism, three or four centuries of Greco-Latin tradition. (Lyotard 1948: 2053)

Political commitment is found in its more traditional form in Lyotard's militant phase, in his writings for the militant journal

Socialisme ou Barbarie on Algeria, collected later in the book *La Guerre des Algériens* (as a young man Lyotard taught in a lycée in Constantine, Algeria). He argues there on the side of the Algerian and French working classes and works for a just overcoming of French colonial rule in Algeria. What is sought is a just resolution for all Algerians, not only for a surrogate ruling class still in the pay of Gaullist France and the USA or for a totalitarian resolution plummeting Algeria into misery and tyranny: 'the problem posed by this deep decomposition of activities and ideals is exactly to know where, by what means the revolutionary project can be expressed, organized, fought.' Yet even here a problematic situation calls for a rethinking of the political against a prevalent militant ideology:

> A certain idea of politics is dying in this society. For sure, the 'democrati-zation' of the regime called for by out-of-work politickers, or the creation of a 'great unified socialist party' that would only be the regrouping of the scraps of the left, will not bring that idea back to life. All that is without perspective, tiny when compared to the size of the crisis. Now is the time for revolutionaries to size up to the revolution we need. (Lyotard 1989a: 196)

Lyotard's political commitment is developed in his two major books *Libidinal Economy* and *The Differend*, where he puts forward philoso-phies offering an alternative to, or a critique of, the traditional con-ception of the political. In particular, these offer the possibility of a political act that does not depend on universal measures and values. Such universality is seen to be dependent on types of representation that seek to account for all aspects of society in a general theory: totalizing discourses and metanarratives. According to him, these are suspect because they threaten to cancel the differences they seek to describe and incorporate. A legal system based on universal human rights may be unjust because its definition of the human may be inconsistent with some of the people or individuals it is applied to. If a standard Western set of practices and values is taken as the template for universal human rights this may lead to great injustice when it is applied to individuals who do not share that Western religious, cul-tural and economic basis. Lyotard's philosophy reminds us of the fundamental importance of difference in the face of totalization. It also seeks to spur us into action on the side of difference and against the unjust application of universal standards and values. Finally, it sets about these two aims in the most appropriate manner: a rich and multifaceted enquiry into science, art, politics, language and ethics where no field dominates and all contribute to our feel for difference.

2

Lyotard's Materialism

Theory and practice

Very few acts serving to change or preserve the world escape doubt. Each action can fail in the most miserable and unforeseen manner. Often the very injustice that we seek to set right returns as a consequence of our actions. This risk is all the stronger where a radical philosophy of action is put forward. How can Lyotard's rethinking of the political escape such risks and doubts? Has he taken the right approach? Is his politics just, as he sometimes claims (and sometimes denies)? Is it realistic? Does it conform to the facts?

The first step towards a resolution of the doubts that plague the philosopher of action is the classification of the questions of the sceptic or doubter into those which are fundamental and those which follow on from them: which obstacles or objections need to be tackled and which can be ignored? For example, is it more important to know what a just action is, or what actions will be possible? Is it more important to know what it is to be good in all cases, or is it more important to know how a specific society operates? The key will be to answer the fundamental questions and to show how then the secondary ones fall by the wayside. The difference between the philosopher of action or commitment and other activists is in the efforts of the former to seek out and answer the fundamental questions. What is sought, therefore, is the greatest degree of certainty as opposed to conviction. This is the philosophical desire to know the outcome, the justice and the justification of an act at the outset, or at least to know that no greater knowledge of them is possible for a given set of circumstances. This arrogance and determination of the philosopher in the face of events determines the individuality of philosophy, as opposed to religion or party politics. How this determination comes to take shape in the writing of a given philosopher serves to define an individual philosophy.

With Lyotard, philosophy of action and commitment finds a new form and a new relevance through a reference to the events which have come to mark his time. He brings the political act up to date and matches it again to the events and society of the second half of the twentieth century. The merit and value of Lyotard's philosophy lies in a timely approach to the philosophical resolution of the sceptical, wise or doubting objections to political action. He is one of the rare philosophers to live up to the new demands of this century. He does so by formulating a new classification of the fundamental and the secondary questions to be addressed and answered by the philosopher of action. The innovation is one of form and of content, that is, he alters how philosophy operates and what is said through the operation.

For example, first, the form of political action is changed by focusing philosophy on the actual state of the society we live in, independent of any prior philosophical theory as to the state it should be in or could be in. Lyotard is not interested in ideals or abstractions but in the matter at hand. In this he can be called a materialist as opposed to an idealist.

Second, the content is altered in so far as the particular description of this state is itself an innovation. Lyotard gives our society new names which overthrow the modern understanding of human and progressive states regulated according to universal values and laws, and replaces them with a feel for states where irresolvable conflicts and differences appear and disappear according to inhuman drives and processes. For example, he calls the world 'libidinal economic', where society is defined as an economy exploiting and releasing desires and feelings – a fitting description of a capitalist society. He is also one of the first to call society 'postmodern' where the description corresponds to a fractured society with no single common aim – thereby capturing our lack of direction and the proliferation of ends in our society of interest groups with no common interest. The content of Lyotard's philosophy involves a new understanding of society in terms of the possibility of political action in it. The terms libidinal economic and postmodern describe it in the light of the will to rethink the values and norms of modern political action.

Why is it such an innovation to concentrate on the actual state of society at a given time in order to be able to formulate political acts within the society? How does Lyotard's turn towards the accurate description of the operation of our society introduce a crucial change in the way we think of political action? After all, it is perhaps more surprising to think of philosophers planning political acts without taking the place where they are to act as fundamental. How can we know how to act, or even understand what action could be, without a reference to the terrain on which the action must take place and due to which action is necessary or desirable?

In fact, few philosophers speak of action without reference to the terrain, to the society where the action must take place, but many do not take that reference as fundamental. Though a commitment to political action is often a central concern in philosophy, it is not the case that this concern holds sway over all others. Where politicians and activists have a direct involvement in the matters of their day, philosophers work in a more abstract context (though this does not mean that they cannot be political activists or active in politics). Thus a concern with political action can be seen as related to other philosophical pursuits that are not directly to do with the actual state of society. The search for the meaning of truth and absolute certainty can be seen as a more properly philosophical concern than an immediate commitment to a given matter at hand. Furthermore, it may be of more value in the long term to determine the way to certainty in action in the abstract than it is to act in accordance with a description of a given matter at hand.

Thus, according to this last view, the questions 'What is certainty?' or 'What is truth?' take sway over the question 'What is going on?' The possibility of a more fundamental field of enquiry than the terrain, than the matter at hand, has now been raised. The study of the actual state of our society will now be considered to be fundamental and primary only if certainty or truth comes to be based on that study. If other fields promise greater dividends in terms of certainty, then they will be taken as the fundamental areas of study and the reference to an actual state of society will come later and will be conditioned by the findings in that primary field.

There are two classic examples of such cases: the appeal to reason and the appeal to conscience as the fundamental aspects of any act within society. In the first case, what is noted is that any consideration of the question arising prior to the political act is based on our thought, the thinking process we go through in order to come to conclusions regarding action. Therefore, certainty must be sought first in the way we think – our reason. If the way we think can provide us with guidelines for achieving the greatest degree of certainty, then it must be there that philosophy concentrates its efforts. The form taken by our thought will determine how we are to act with the greatest degree of certainty, the principle will be what it is rational to do in any case (our standard use of the principle of applying a pseudo-logical 'common sense' fits this model well). The terrain on which we have to act will become a secondary matter because we will have overriding principles that provide for the greatest degree of certainty independent of where they have to be applied.

Similarly, a philosophy taking conscience as its foundation has asked the question of why we are seeking to act. It has come up, say, with the answer 'To do good'. The fundamental question then becomes 'What is the good?' Again, if an answer can be found to this question independent of specific situations, then the philosophy will have fundamental principles at its disposal. The principle, for example, that the good is dictated by our conscience in all cases could then override the consideration of a given terrain, that is, no given state of society could render the principle of following our conscience invalid. Therefore, the philosophy taking the good as determined by conscience or the true as determined by reason as its basis offers a theory and foundation for our consideration of action prior to a given material state of society.

Lyotard's philosophy is in direct opposition to this position. It puts the terrain first and, consequently, any philosophical thought on political action is a practical study of what is and is not possible and what is and is not good and just on the given terrain. There are no universal principles here, there is no transcendent idea, no idea independent of an experience of the good or the true rising above specific cases but applicable to them. The theoretical study of conscience or rationality is replaced by a practical philosophy that starts with the study of the society or terrain in which it must operate, only then to pass on to the study of the possible, the true and the good within that society.

It is important, though, to realize that this matter is not a familiar commonsense view of society. Rather, Lyotard stretches the definition of society to include it in a much stranger underlying matter. In one case, the matter is libidinal; in another, it is linguistic. The form of Lyotard's philosophy is therefore antifoundational, in the sense that it is opposed to the search for certain foundations (ideals and principles) for action independent of a given state of affairs. Instead, we are given a materialist philosophy where the emphasis is on the state of society now, *the matter at hand*. Thus Lyotard's materialist accounts of society will be the first topic to be focused on in this study, in chapters 3 and 4. In these chapters, his accounts of the postmodern state and the libidinal-economic state will be presented and explained as the terrain in which political action must take place.

A critical defence

It is not enough, though, merely to put the study of a given state of society first. Two strong and related objections can be raised against such an approach; both are formal philosophical objections and they accuse the approach of being itself unphilosophical. The first, specific, objection raises the point that there are foundations that come prior to the study of this matter at hand and these are the proper first topic for philosophy. This objection asks the question 'How can you be certain that the study of the terrain is the primary way towards the greatest certainty in action?' The second, general, objection raises the point that the study of the matter at hand must itself necessarily be based on a foundation independent of it; objectors ask the question 'How can you be certain that the way you study the terrain is the most certain way?'

The arguments turn on the demand for philosophy to search for the maximum degree of certainty before passing on to the consideration of political action. They argue that for a philosophy to take any relative state as the key topic of study is to bypass the search for certainty. This, then, implies a lack of difference between a philosophy taking the matter at hand as its primary study topic and those political pursuits, such as party politics, that avoid the search for the maximum degree of certainty. This is a strong accusation: on an emotive basis, it raises the risk of the end of philosophy brought on from within philosophy itself through its dissolution into other subjects – an act of treachery; on a logical basis, that is, on the basis of a demand for consistency, it raises the problem of how the term philosophy can be used if it cannot be differentiated from mere party politics or political opinion. These objections carry considerable force against some aspects of Lyotard's philosophy.

In particular, *The Postmodern Condition* can be interpreted as merely a weak – though timely – study of a particular historical moment. According to this view, the book would fail as an objective survey, because it does not pay adequate attention to the many areas implicated in its wide-ranging hypothesis. On this count, critics could point to deeper and more specialized studies of a given topic. For example, though it addresses the problem of the legitimation of science, *The Postmodern Condition* does not engage directly with the work of philosophers of science such as Popper, Kuhn or Feyerabend. Neither, though, does it undertake an extensive empirical study of contemporary scientific practices. Thus philosophers in the analytic tradition are bound to find Lyotard's approach surprising, if not simply wrong. Richard Rorty, for example, finds Lyotard's arguments on postmodern science 'odd' and 'invalid': 'Lyotard argues invalidly from the current concerns of various scientific disciplines to the claim that science is somehow discovering that it should aim at permanent revolution, rather than at the alternation between normality and revolution made familiar by Kuhn' (1991: 165-6).

The second objection claims that Lyotard's own argument involves a crisis of legitimation, that is, it is impossible for Lyotard to legitimate his own thesis on the impossibility of universally legitimate arguments. This point is made in Fredric Jameson's foreword to the English translation of *The Postmodern Condition*: '[*The Postmodern Condition*] becomes a symptom of the state it seeks to diagnose' (1984: xi). According to this view, Lyotard would be unable to demonstrate his point without at the same time proving that it is false. (Jameson, though, believes that it is possible to escape this serious challenge to the possibility of truth in philosophical argument through an appeal to 'unconscious master-narratives' (pp. x–xi). A great many critics of Lyotard make similar criticisms by accusing Lyotard of falling victim to a performative contradiction (see Manfred Frank's points in chapter 8 below).

Against these objections Lyotard affirms that philosophy must deduce its understanding of the true and the good from within the study of a matter at hand, and there is an error whenever there is a pursuit of the good and the true independent of it. The matter at hand is the prior topic for any philosophy: to seek foundations elsewhere and then to return ready armed to act on the matter at hand is to misunderstand that matter. Here, because the way of greatest certainty is materialist and not idealist, abstract ideas and theories do not apply to a given material state and, therefore, they cannot be the ground for the deduction of the greatest certainty in action; such certainty can only be achieved through the study of an actual state of society. The price to pay for this shift from the ideal to the material will be a corresponding shift in the role of certainty in philosophy. For Lyotard, certainty becomes relative to the matter at hand and, hence, he risks losing any claims to absolute certainty. In fact, Lyotard revels in this risk since it marks the possible defeat of those who seek the absolute.

This important retort and argument is an intrinsic part of Lyotard's studies of the libidinal-economic and postmodern states. It is developed from within those studies and argues against the two criticisms given above. The argument has two strands; they make up the second essential aspect of Lyotard's philosophy and offer a further reason for its importance within contemporary philosophy. In the first strand, there is a response to the specific form of the argument as it can be inferred from the philosophies of Hegel and Marx, in one version, and in a completely different and opposed version, the line of thinkers who depart from phenomenology (the philosophy and ethics of Emmanuel Levinas, in particular). The term version must be stressed here because, on many counts, these philosophers cannot be associated with an understanding of philosophy as independent of a given actual state of society. In Lyotard's philosophy they can and it is exactly because they appear to avoid this error but in fact do not that they are chosen as the most serious adversaries to the Lyotard position.

In the second strand, the general argument for foundations other than in the study of an actual state of society is responded to through the practical presentation of the counter-argument: 'How can we know that the way of greatest certainty must have foundations determined independently of the study of specific states, without having to refer to a specific state?' That is, the demand for foundations independent of the matter at hand is itself made from within a matter at hand or particular state of society, which must be studied before we can fully understand the demand. Here, Lyotard's argument shows how impossible it is to abstract from the particular and that therefore the argument calling for such an abstraction is void. This critical element of Lyotard's thought situates him within the poststructuralist reaction of the late 1960s. There, the emergence of new ways of thinking about politics, language, art and society involved an implicit critique of dialectics, structuralism and phenomenology (and hence existentialism). Thus the positive approach of Lyotard's philosophy and its critical elements have a shared destiny. Weaknesses in the former damage the latter. Many attacks on Lyotard point out the contradictions of his single-minded commitment to the matter at hand, in order to return philosophical and political thought to a possible deduction of universal norms from practical observations.

Questions of strategy

Up to this point, I have discussed the framework in which Lyotard's philosophy is to be understood. The framework consists of three central aspects: first, a philosophical rethinking of the political; second, the approach through the prior study of an actual state of society – I have called this the study of the matter at hand; and third, the defence of that approach through a critique of the philosophical arguments and positions offering alternatives to Lyotard's primary commitment to the study of the matter at hand. The next step in this understanding of Lyotard's work involves an analysis of Lyotard's response to a pair of further critical questions. The first question asks what method is to be used in the study of the actual state of society, that is, 'How are we to give an account of the actual state of society?'; and the second asks what practical answers this study brings to the question 'How should we act?' or 'How should we act in this society?'

Neither question, though, returns to the demand for a foundation outside the study of the matter at hand; they assume, with Lyotard, that no such foundation must be given. However, this concession does nothing to blunt their critical power. Instead, it focuses their attack on *strategic considerations* within a philosophy directed at political action. This request for an account of Lyotard's methodology and practical politics rejoins his most severe critics. He has often been opposed and dismissed on the grounds that his methodology is unsound and that consequently his politics are ineffective or reactionary.

The term 'strategic considerations' introduces two presuppositions to philosophical argument: the first is an agreement with a set terrain or field of action, in this case the study of the actual state of society and the goal of being able to act politically in the terrain. The second is an agreement that the methods and goals to be used on the terrain are open to discussion in terms of how they fit an overall strategy aimed at achieving an ultimate goal. The strategic questions resemble those asked by a commander prior to a campaign. The commander knows the terrain and knows that the ultimate goal is to win the campaign, but two further questions remain. The first, 'Given all the possible courses of action available to me now, which one is the best to take in these circumstances?', is put to the commander. This question seeks to guarantee the outcome of the campaign as far as is possible. The second question, 'What are the specific political goals of the campaign?', is put to the politicians. The answer to this question is important in determining the acceptable costs of the campaign; for example, it may be militarily expedient, but politically suicidal in the long term, to massacre all uncooperative civilians. Without answers to these questions the commander's action will be doomed to political or military failure – unless blessed with immense good fortune.

Like the commander, the political philosopher undertaking a study of an actual state of society with a view to rethinking political action within that society must answer these two crucial strategic questions: 'What method to use in the study of the society?' and 'What precisely is the philosophical direction that guides this study?' It is important, here, to stress that these are now strategic questions and not fundamental questions, that is, they are asked in the context of given presuppositions, in the context of a particular study, and not as the foundation to studies in general. The underlying questions have now become 'What path promises the best chance of success in this case?' and 'What is success in this case?'; these have replaced the fundamental question put earlier, 'What is certainty?' Lyotard's philosophy must address these underlying questions. This is because, in accepting an actual state of society as its primary study topic and in accepting the political act as the ultimate goal of the study, his philosophy has become strategic: what is sought by Lyotard is the strategic solution to a challenge on a particular terrain. The questions of method and of specific goals are therefore all-important in any understanding and judgement of his philosophy. The claim to rethink the political and the attempt to describe the matter at hand for this rethinking, involve specific methods and outcomes which form a large part of Lyotard's philosophical impact.

Chapter 5 of the book will cover Lyotard's method and chapter 6 will cover the specific goals of his philosophy, as they emerge from within his study of the actual state of society and his critical reflection on the political. These chapters serve to explain the better-known aspects of his philosophy, his description of states of society and his critique of idealist philosophies. Chapter 5 shows the different philosophical methods that lead Lyotard to the libidinal economy and the postmodern condition; it also provides a context whereby criticisms of his accounts of the matter at hand can be taken further and answered in terms of the philosophical thinking behind them. Chapter 6 shows the specific goals set for the philosopher of action in the libidinal economy and in the postmodern condition, after the abandonment of other, more traditional conceptions of political action; it provides a context for a critical survey of the practical politics coming out of Lyotard's philosophy.

It is important to note, though, that any appeal to Lyotard's methods or specific goals is not final because they are themselves strategic responses to a given state of affairs. The lack of an absolute foundation leads the philosophy into a circular development: it starts with a matter at hand, that determines a strategic approach, that determines a methodology, that studies the matter at hand, the study understanding the matter at hand further, this determining the strategy anew, and so on . . .

This problematic circularity leads to a split in the critical evaluations of Lyotard's philosophy. On the one hand, there is the evaluation based on a criticism of the circularity in the development of Lyotard's philosophy. On the other hand, there is the critical evaluation that accepts the circularity of Lyotard's approach. The first critical evaluation is an attack on Lyotard's whole approach to the resolution of the problem of political action. It returns to the demand for foundations independent of a given matter at hand by making the point that the circularity inhibits any judgement as to the certainty of Lyotard's philosophy. The question here is 'If Lyotard's philosophy is in constant change, at which point in the circle do we judge the validity of Lyotard's philosophy?' This criticism will be dealt with in chapter 8 of the book (in particular, where there is a summary of the critical points made by the philosophers Jacques Derrida, Gilles Deleuze and Manfred Frank, among others).

In the second critical evaluation, a judgement is made in terms of specific strategic considerations, thereby accepting that Lyotard's strategy is open to amendment and change. In effect, such an evaluation enters into a debate with Lyotard as to what is the best course of action to take in given circumstances – it says 'There is a better way of doing this.' This will be the main critical approach of this book. The more radical evaluation given above refuses to accept the ground for such a debate – it says 'This is completely the wrong approach.'

The studies in chapters 5 and 6 complete the presentation of the key issues put forward by Lyotard. He is an important and influential philosopher because of his analyses of the actual state of our society, because of his critique of other important philosophical arguments, but also because his philosophical methods and goals are original responses to the problem of understanding the actual state of society and to the challenge of developing political acts in that society. Thus, besides the description of society as libidinal economical and besides the critique of, among others, Marxist philosophy and politics, *Libidinal Economy* also reintroduces a materialist philosophical method that can be traced back to Spinoza and Nietzsche. Put simply, the method involves the description of systems as economies regulating the flow of feelings and desires. Similarly, *The Differend* not only completes Lyotard's description of the postmodern condition and criticizes the philosophies of Hegel and Levinas and many others, it sets out a novel philosophy of language and a development of the Kantian theory of sublime feelings – feelings so strong that they overwhelm our capacity to rationalize them.

Thus we find that for Lyotard the political and social are understood in terms of the concatenation of phrases and the rules governing the way one sentence is linked to another (these involve what Lyotard calls phrase universes, regimens and genres):

> 198. It could be said that the social is given immediately with a phrase universe (be it the one presented by the tail of a cat), and that it is given as immediately determined by, in principle, the regimen of the phrase, even though its determination is straightaway the determination of another phrase, whose linking on cannot help but be the occasion of differends between genres of discourse. It could be said for that very reason that politics is immediately given with a phrase as a differend to be regulated concerning the matter of the means of linking on to it. (1988a: 140–1)

In *The Differend*, political action is presented as a response to intense, sublime feelings such as extreme enthusiasm (explained in the following passage in terms of Lyotard's interpretation of Kant's political philosophy – the act is Kant's deduction of the possibility of progress towards the better for the human race, the enthusiasm belongs to spectators of the French revolution):

> In this way, the enthusiasm which betrays itself on the occasion of the French Revolution, first because it is an extreme feeling of the sublime, then because this feeling already requires a formal culture of skill, and finally because this culture in turn has civil and perhaps international peace as its horizon – this enthusiasm itself – 'not only permits people to hope for progress towards the better, but is already itself progress in so far as its capacity is sufficient for the present' (*Conflict*, s. 6). (Lyotard 1988a: 166; see also Kant 1990)

Limits of representation, events, absolute difference and the avant-garde

Lyotard is an original and obsessive philosopher. Throughout his work he has returned to particular themes again and again in an attempt to do justice to them in a philosophical context. This obsession is understood best in the context of the rethinking of the political in a politically committed materialist philosophy, rather than as a psychological or autobiographical trait. Lyotard returns to a given theme to mark a variation in his reflection on the political. Therefore, in parallel to the study of the structure of Lyotard's philosophy, to the pursuit of his arguments, methods and goals, it is helpful to plot the development of the themes that make Lyotard's poststructuralist philosophy unique and original, that make him influential in terms of the specific ideas he gives to a philosophical movement.

Lyotard's influence in fields outside academic philosophy, in modern art or in literary and political theory for example, is due as much to these recurrent themes, and to the theories which give them form, as it is to his overall philosophical approach. Literary theorists, political and legal thinkers, artists and thinkers in the field of aesthetics (philosophers of art but also museum curators and exhibition organizers) have taken up the ideas developed around the attempt to formulate a political philosophy. Lyotard has become an important figure in aesthetics, cultural studies and literary theory; his work provides a basis for new and productive forms of criticism, interpretation and creativity.

For example, Bill Readings has developed an elegant analysis of Werner Herzog's film *Where the Green Ants Dream* around the question of the encounter of the law of the colonialist and Aboriginal life in Australia. Readings uses Lyotard's reflection on absolute difference and the limits of representation to consider the question of justice, where the Aboriginals are judged by a law that cannot recognize the legitimacy of their ways of life:

> In Herzog's treatment of the Aboriginal in the face of the law, injustice is shown to reside not in the accidents or errors of the political or legal representation of rights nor in a particular structure of political or legal representation but in the exclusive rule of representation itself. (Readings 1992: 172)

Here the crossover between Lyotard's thought, art and politics is made explicit. What is interesting is that the development of the theme of the limits of representation allows for a wide variety of applications. Each one adds to the richness of the theme; while the theme provides a strong philosophical support for the political analysis of a work of art. It is therefore useful to explain this influence through a presentation of the main themes of his philosophy in terms of a central philosophical structure. This is because the impact of these themes is due as much to their wider philosophical and political dimension, and the way in which they come to be developed in Lyotard's libidinal philosophy and philosophy of language, as it is to the individual interest aroused by the theme.

A notable by-product of this extended interest in Lyotard's work is the extensive and prompt availability of his work in translation. He has been well served by a number of excellent translators. Each translation is based on a firm grasp of Lyotard's philosophy and philosophical questions in general and the outcome is nearly always satisfactory in terms of style and precision. Perhaps the most outstanding achievement is Iain Hamilton Grant's recent translation of *Économie libidinale* (Lyotard 1993a), given the pyrotechnical style yet complex argument of the book.

Themes provide the thread that not only joins Lyotard's many journal articles and minor books together, but also joins these articles to the central books *Libidinal Economy* and *The Differend*. In most of these articles and books he develops ideas around one or more of them as the way to understand a given problem or topic. The four most important themes will be covered in this book. They are the limits of representation; the event; absolute difference; and the avantgarde. In each of these, Lyotard leaves a legacy of deep and insightful formulations of traditional philosophical problems, in the context of a critical reflection on the search for relevant political acts. It is important, here, to draw a distinction between the observation of the themes which run through his work, and their development at particular stages. For example, the *theme* of the event can be traced through most of the work but the theoretical framework used to account for it varies greatly (see Bennington 1988). At this stage, I will give general characterizations of them, deferring an explanation of their precise development to later.

The limits of representation This theme marks Lyotard's interest in the limits of the various means we have for the representation of things, such as language and art. It has always been a concern of Lyotard's that there may be things that cannot be represented, that is, brought back to us through language or art. This means that our powers of representation are limited and that our thought – dependent on the representation of things – falls short of our senses and feelings. These, on the other hand, attend the immediate presentation of the thing, its occurrence. This concern shows up in Lyotard's earliest writings; in 'Nés en 1925', for example, Lyotard noted the inability of language and art to represent their subject:

> [After the war] Actions are removed from goals, projects are free of ambition, to undertake a project, to accomplish an action are now self-validating motions. In parallel, art has abandoned figure, the represented has drowned in representation; Raphael bores us. Objects have gone through the same liberation process as the goals of concrete projects, surrealist expression has accustomed us to works where signification is left to chance, that is, where man has never been more free. (Lyotard 1948: 2050)

The event   Lyotard calls this immediate occurrence of the thing beyond the powers of representation an event. The event also appears in Lyotard's earliest works and grows in importance to become his trademark. Through his thought on it, Lyotard has emphasized the philosophical importance of those things that happen to us, that we experience, and that move us, and yet that we cannot think through in language or in art (although art itself may constitute one such event). For Lyotard, events are all-important paradoxes, occurrences which we cannot think adequately. They are the way to a humility of reason and rationality. Take, for example, the role of the event in *Libidinal Economy*, where he attacks any effort to compare libidinal intensities or any attempt to represent them:

> And all the comparisons which may come to mind, they are damned in advance by the accumulation (*cum*) which they comprise and which subject them to procedures of weighing, thought, commensurability, good for the register and accountability, for ever incapable of yielding intensity in its *event*. (Lyotard 1993a: 18)

Lyotard has always been interested in these occurrences that go beyond our powers of representation; he calls them events.

Absolute difference   The limits of representation, as shown through events, curtail the power of thought. In particular, if the occurrence of all things exceeds representation, then the capacity of thought to compare, contrast, classify and categorize events is curtailed. Thought can no longer be a bridge between different things, between individual people, works of art, ways of life, cultural artefacts, desires and so on. The impossibility of this intellectual bridge introduces the theme of absolute difference. Lyotard holds that cultures, works of art, ways of life, people, desires cannot be compared because as events, as things that occur, they are absolutely different from one another. In *The Differend*, he uses the term heterogeneity to express this difference and this barrier to reason (note the barrier also stands against the power of capital, for example, when comparisons are set up between things through prices); what is more, the most important term of Lyotard's late philosophy, the differend, depends on this absolute difference:

> 263. The only insurmountable obstacle that the hegemony of the economic genre comes up against is the heterogeneity of phrase regimens and of genres of discourse. This is because there is not 'language' and 'Being', but occurrences. The obstacle does not depend on the 'will' of human beings in one sense or in another, but upon the differend. (Lyotard 1988a: 181)

The avant-garde   The themes of the event and absolute difference involve a paradox, an absurd situation (a paradox that plagues all Lyotard's works whenever these themes are returned to). The theme of the avant-garde is Lyotard's response to this paradox. It can be raised, first, through the question 'How can we discuss that which cannot be discussed, that which is beyond representation – the event?' and, second, through the query 'How can you know that two things are absolutely different if you cannot compare them?' Throughout his work Lyotard uses the avant-garde or the example of avant-garde artists to show how we can live with this paradox. According to him avant-garde art attempts to represent that which cannot be represented. For example, in the essay 'The sublime and the avant-garde' (in *The Lyotard Reader*) Lyotard links his work on the sublime feeling to the event or occurrence and to the ability of the truly avant-garde, as opposed to mere innovators, to 'express' occurrence:

> The occurrence, the *Ereignis* [event], has nothing to do with the *petit frisson*, the cheap thrill, the profitable pathos, that accompanies an innovation. Hidden in the cynicism of innovation is certainly the despair that nothing further will happen. But innovation means to behave as though lots of things happened, and to make them happen. Through innovation, the will affirms its hegemony over time. . . . With occurrence the will is defeated. The avant-gardist task remains that of undoing the presumption of the mind with respect to time. The sublime feeling is the name of this privation. (Lyotard 1989b: 210–11)

This theme of the avant-garde as the saying of that which cannot be said then leads, in *The Differend*, to the definition of the task of the philosopher as the search for 'impossible' idioms for the phrasing of irresolvable conflicts involving absolute differences (differends): 'In coddling the event, one puts on a Horrorshow *à la Grand Guignol*. One's responsibility before thought consists, on the contrary, in detecting differends and in finding the (impossible) idiom for phrasing them. This is what a philosopher does' (Lyotard 1988a: 142).

The development of the important themes given above will be covered in each of the following chapters when the central structure of Lyotard's philosophy reflects on them. This will allow an understanding of Lyotard's philosophy in terms of its recurring and influential aspects; it will also allow an explanation of the key ideas of the philosophy, in terms of the central recurring structure of themes, and in terms of the methods and specific goals of the philosophy.

Lyotard's rethinking of the political through these central themes, and the well-defined concepts that come to be associated with them, keep his philosophy in constant touch with its prior motive in the political act. Thereby he avoids the danger of excessive scholasticism or professionalism, where the scholarship and the profession have become unwanted or irrelevant in a particular society. However, in so doing, Lyotard runs another risk: the risk of missing important lessons from the past, either in terms of the understanding of the actual state of society or in terms of the methods and specific goals of philosophy. The danger is that Lyotard could be a bad philosopher as opposed to an irrelevant one – bad in the sense of lacking in philosophical knowledge, or bad in the sense of making unnecessary philosophical mistakes, that is, mistakes that have been made before. The latter flaw is the most serious since it involves unnecessary errors and hence avoidable practical disasters; the former only involves an inefficient use of philosophical resources.

In practice, however, Lyotard cannot be accused of being an inefficient philosopher because his philosophy makes constant references to the history of philosophy. Whenever such a reference seems to provide his work with a short-cut for the solution to a strategic problem, or whenever a philosophy from the past offers an insight on the development of the actual state of society, Lyotard does not hesitate to undertake a study of that philosophy. On the contrary, he is a plunderer, prepared to dive into the work of Kant or Marx or Freud or Nietzsche or Wittgenstein whenever he detects something that may be of use. This reference to past philosophies does not, though, shelter Lyotard from the more serious accusation of making unnecessary mistakes due to a disregard for the lessons of the past. Worse, it is possible that his efficient eclecticism could be interpreted as mistaken expediency: the plundering of the past for its ideas but with no regard for the errors associated with those ideas or with their misuse.

For example, the attack outlined above in the section on Lyotard's critical philosophy (see p. 11) on the lack of foundations in Lyotard's work could be made from the point of view of philosophers working in the Kantian tradition. They could accuse Lyotard of neglecting the foundations of Kant's philosophy when he appeals to Kant's concept of the sublime in the philosophy of *The Differend*. In itself, this would not be a serious accusation, but in conjunction with a demonstration that this oversight led to a mistaken understanding of the actual state of society and of the methods and goals to be used when dealing with such a society this would be a damning indictment of Lyotard's approach.

In order to give due regard to these criticisms of Lyotard's philosophy, the final chapter of the book will refer to the main critical attacks on it. Attacks will be selected because they combine a critical reading of the philosophical basis to Lyotard's philosophy with an opposition to its methods and specific goals. This combination amounts to a criticism of Lyotard's understanding of the actual state of society, and of the action to be taken in that society, together with an explanation of the philosophical errors leading to the mistaken understanding and action. Three philosophical schools will be studied: deconstruction and the possible deconstruction of Lyotard's later philosophy, as performed in the work of Jacques Derrida; the Habermasian critique related to the work of Jürgen Habermas and the Frankfurt School; and the more sympathetic and productive commentary in parallel to Lyotard's early work, by Gilles Deleuze and Félix Guattari. The first two critiques can be understood as two very different reactions to the problem of circularity in Lyotard's philosophy, that is, to the problem of whether any certainty can be based on a study of a matter at hand that itself lacks a basis. Why are Lyotard's materialist strategies and specific goals more certain than others? The third reading, on the other hand, pushes the limits of Lyotard's libidinal economics and tends towards an even more radical materialism. This move then presents an opposing position to Lyotard's later work, thereby providing us with a counter to the development of his philosophy.

3

States of Society: the Postmodern Condition

General features of the postmodern condition

Lyotard's philosophy first reached a wider academic audience outside France through his 'report on knowledge', *The Postmodern Condition*, a description of the cultural state of highly developed societies, commissioned by the government of Quebec:

> The object of this study is the condition of knowledge in the most highly developed societies. I have decided to use the word postmodern to describe that condition. The word is in current use on the American continent among sociologists and critics; it designates the state of our culture following the transformations which, since the end of the nineteenth century, have altered the game rules for science, literature and the arts. The present study will place these transformations in the context of the crisis of narratives. (1984b: xxiii)

The postmodern condition deals directly with familiar terms from our social environment: the linguistic structures we use in various forms of communication and, by the time these structures are thought out fully, in *The Differend*, the powerful feelings that condition the way we communicate and act.

The modest form chosen by Lyotard, a report, belies the vastness and difficulty of his project: a report on knowledge, science, literature and the arts in the twentieth century. Yet the scale and breadth of the undertaking is typical of his thought and concerns. Lyotard wants to show two apparently contradictory things. First, he argues that it is possible to consider science, literature and the arts in terms of a single concept, 'postmodern'. Second, he wants to argue that these fields cannot be reconciled according to a single account of their positive interrelation, in terms of progress towards the emancipation of mankind, for example. This means that Lyotard must select a single method of analysis that allows him to analyse a series of different fields. But it also means that this method must not itself point to an overall unity of the fields in terms of goals, rules and values. The method he devises to solve this problem is the study of the linguistic accounts that are deployed in different fields. In particular, he is interested in the narratives that are used to justify the validity of statements within fields: why a particular statement is true, important and ultimately worthwhile.

His aim is to show that these narratives allow us to define rule-governed practices that coincide with the fields of science, literature and the arts, and many others. The narrative on truth, norms and goals defines how the 'game' of art or science should be played. Hence Lyotard's profound interest in borrowing Ludwig Wittgenstein's term 'language game' (Wittgenstein 1953). He will use the study of language games to achieve the seemingly impossible task of surveying knowledge in the twentieth century. The claim that these fields can be analysed in terms of language games draws them together. However, that unity is then blown apart by the second aspect of Lyotard's project. He attempts to show that there is no overall narrative that can give us overarching rules between fields. For example, we find that the rules of science and art cannot be reconciled. This is his famous disbelief in metanarratives. It is justified through an argument for the incommensurability of language games. By incommensurability Lyotard means that there is no common set of rules, norms and values between games. Thus the aim to define the postmodern condition becomes a linguistic project on language games, narratives and metanarratives. The fragmentation and loss of shared values characteristic of postmodernity becomes the incommensurability of language games and the disbelief in metanarratives.

So the postmodern condition is first described in terms of a multiplicity of language games, where language games are linguistic practices defined by particular rules. There are many different language games and these enter into conflict with one another over what proper practice is in given cases. In a language game, 'various categories of utterance can be defined in terms of rules specifying their properties and the uses to which they can be put – in exactly the same way as the game of chess is defined by a set of rules determining the properties of each of the pieces, in other words, the proper way to move them' (Lyotard 1984b: 10). Proper practice is set by the rules of each language game, that is, language games justify moves within them by referring to rules. Secondly, Lyotard is particularly interested in justification and the way in which a justification from within one language game is absolutely incompatible with a justification from within another. This property leads Lyotard to his well-known and controversial disbelief in metanarratives, that is, language games that reconcile conflicting language games within a single overarching view.

An illustration of the postmodern condition could be a city divided into quarters. Each quarter has its laws (language game) and these laws are what gives it its identity. For example, one quarter could have laws based on property, another could have laws based on class and another could have laws based on strength and sex. Legal problems arise in the city in cases where a 'crime' takes place on the boundary between quarters. In such cases a judgement according to the laws of one quarter will offend the inhabitants of another. What makes this city postmodern is that there is no way of avoiding these conflicts between quarters; neither is there any way of resolving the conflicts in a manner that is acceptable to all the sides. In the postmodern city, there is no possibility of a benevolent ruler uniting all the quarters under one just law. Instead, in order to bring peace to the city, such a ruler will have to subjugate some or all of the quarters.

In the postmodern condition, it is impossible to reconcile two different language games in such a way as to do justice to both; Lyotard calls this the incommensurability of language games. When incommensurable language games come into dispute over a given case, he says there is a differend, an irresolvable conflict between them. The main point to retain about differends is that they cannot be resolved in fairness to both of the games involved. This incommensurability becomes apparent to us through a feeling, the feeling of the sublime. The feeling occurs where the rules of a particular language game are applied to a case unjustly; it allows us, therefore, to recognize conflicts that take place at the boundaries of language games. For example, the absolute incompatibility of the language game that allows a move preaching the sanctity of life and the language game that allows a move advocating equal retribution is revealed when we experience the conjunction of feelings of revenge (aroused by a gruesome murder) and pity (aroused by the mechanical chill of a state execution).

Lyotard's description of the postmodern condition is aimed at a politics based on the recognition of differends, that is, of conflicts that cannot be resolved equitably. From the point of view of one or the other language game, and from the point of view of the search for a form of justice that aims to take both into account, this politics can seem wrong and dangerous. There is no escaping this moral frustration, since Lyotard puts testimony for the differend above any resolution of it. This has to be the case since, according to Lyotard's philosophy, any resolution must perpetrate a further injustice which cannot be justified as a resolution of the first.

The event in a postmodern context

In *The Postmodern Condition* and *Au Juste* (translated as *Just Gaming*), Lyotard's description of the actual state of society as postmodern has come to replace an earlier description of the libidinal economy. The main feature of this shift is the abandonment of the libidinal description in favour of a description of the relation between justice and language. He has moved to a study of the linguistic structure of different accounts and of how this structure has an effect on what are taken to be just and unjust actions. Three factors are of particular importance here. The first is the linking together – 'concatenation' – of various linguistic elements. Whenever an attempt is made to account for any given event, sentences or phrases must be linked together to form the account. Lyotard investigates the rules that govern this concatenation. In *The Differend* he calls this process the linking of phrases:

> 138. A linkage may reveal an equivocalness in the previous phrase. *The door is closed* can give rise to *Of course, what do you think doors are for?*, or to *I know, they're trying to lock me in*, or to *All the better, I have to talk to you*, etc. In these linkages, the closed door ceases to be a state of things to be discussed or verified. (1988a: 81)

A phrase occurs and we must respond to it, that is, we must link on from the initial phrase. Lyotard studies the rules governing our response and how these rules relate to the general question of what a just response could be. For example, how should we respond to the phrase 'Please help me to die!'? Are there any patterns or rules in the way we use language, in the way we understand the phrase or in the previous responses to such phrases that might help us or force us to respond in a particular way?

The second factor is the way linguistic elements seem to work against or contradict one another in specific cases. Here Lyotard is interested in the possibility of different but equally justified accounts of given events and in the way these contradictory accounts fit together. For example, two religious groups could have different accounts of why a particular plot of land is holy and it may be impossible to verify either account, due to their dependence on the true faith of the adherents to each religion. In *The Postmodern Condition* he calls such an opposition of linguistic elements the incommensurability or heterogeneity of language games: 'There are many different language games – a heterogeneity of elements. They only give rise to institutions in patches – local determinism' (1984b: xxiv). The coexistence or conflict of these elements is called the agonistic of language games (from the Greek *agon* or contest): 'This last observation brings us to the first principle underlying our method as a whole: to speak is to fight, in the sense of playing, and speech acts fall within the domain of a general agonistic' (1984b: 10). Here language is seen as made up of competing language games. Each game must have a set of rules determining the legitimate use of sentences within the game; to modify the set of rules is to change the game: 'even an infinitesimal modification of one rule alters the nature of the game' (1984b: 10). These rules involve the tacit or explicit agreement of those who use the language game; only the agreement gives the rules their legitimacy, that is, there are no rules that are immediately legitimate: 'rules do not carry within themselves their own legitimation.' Finally, in terms of language, every utterance is a move in the game. According to Lyotard, games thus defined enter into conflicts of matters of the legitimate judgement of cases. Questions such as 'Should the case be judged according to the rules of this game or another?' indicate these conflicts.

The Postmodern Condition concentrates on a particular opposition of this kind: the opposition or incommensurability of the language game of scientific knowledge and the language game of narrative knowledge (the stories we tell about ourselves and our society). In the language game of science there are rules as to the admissibility of evidence and as to the correctness of proof. These rules are incompatible with the rules governing narrative knowledge because, for instance, the latter may accept exaggeration and invention without proof. So, in *The Postmodern Condition*, incompossible figures have given way to incommensurable language games or genres, that is, rule-governed forms of communication. Different language games have different rules governing what is a justifiable account of any given event. According to Lyotard, these rules cannot be made to coincide; they have no common measure with respect to the cases they have to judge. The language games or genres they govern are therefore said to be incommensurable. Yet these incompatible accounts have to coexist, they have to enter into disputes over matters in which they have a shared interest. In particular, language games come into conflict over different justifications of a particular event. These conflicts can never be resolved in a way that is just from all points of view, because the rules they have for deciding this matter are absolutely incompatible.

The third factor central to Lyotard's study of language and justice is the question of how to determine what a just account of an event could be – that is, what rules there are to determine whether a particular account is just. This factor is important because it translates Lyotard's concern for the political act into his work on language. He asks: 'What kind of accounts are just accounts of a given event and hence the basis for just political action?' Lyotard's book *Au Juste* investigates the many problems involved in answering this question, and *The Postmodern Condition* is driven by the question of legitimation, that is, 'How do we determine what is a legitimate linguistic response to an event?':

> The question of the legitimacy of science has been indissociably linked to that of the legitimation of the legislator since the time of Plato. From this point of view, the right to decide what is true is not independent of the right to decide what is just, even if the statements consigned by these two authorities differ in nature. The point is that there is a strict interlinkage between the kinds of language called science and the kind called ethics and politics: they both stem from the same perspective, the same 'choice' if you will – the choice called the Occident. (1984b: 8)

The study of justification leads to the definition of different linguistic elements: language games with specific and incommensurable rules governing what is a just act in the language game.

The connection between the earlier philosophy of desire and this later philosophy of language is made through Lyotard's concept of the event. Where feelings are associated with language games or genres, properties of feelings as events dictate two factors concerning justification within language games. First, because events cannot be fully represented, no justification can claim to have a complete understanding of the event; it will therefore always be possible for such a justification to be wrong. Second, because it is possible for occurring events to be beyond the powers of understanding and representation of any given language game, the occurrence of such events can mark the boundary of that game with another incommensurable game. The first factor is a law governing the concatenation or linking of sentences in terms of genres or language games; it says that there is no just way of linking a sentence on to a feeling as event. The second factor follows on from the prior law. The law shows how it is possible for there to be incommensurable language games, that is, because there is no absolutely just concatenation, it is possible for there to be incompatible concatenations that are equally just – but only according to the incommensurable rules of justification of each language game.

The second factor adds a way of detecting the boundaries between language games to this possibility. The boundaries between these language games can be determined according to the feelings that cannot be accounted for from within a particular game. A feeling occurs and brings us to question the rules of a particular language game. At this point a new set of rules is necessary to account for the feeling, to do justice to it. This new set of rules will define a different incommensurable language game. The feelings of grief or angst, for example, may show the limitations of the language game of science on the topic of death. The postmodern condition involves incommensurable language games whose borders are revealed by feelings. When a feeling as event cannot be represented, or made to fit the rules of justification of a particular language game, there must be a limit of the game. What is more, in addition to the existence of incommensurable language games, there is a law that can be applied to all linguistic acts: feelings as events can never be fully justified or represented from within any one language game or genre.

Lyotard's law and incredulity towards metanarratives

The Postmodern Condition puts forward a defence of a statement against the possibility of a certain kind of account of events: the metanarrative. Lyotard states that he does not believe metanarratives, that is, accounts offering a way of bringing together all rules of justification into one overall justification. This involves, for example, an incredulity towards the metanarrative of human emancipation, that is, the story of how the human race has set itself free that brings together the language game of science, the language game of human historical conflicts and the language game of human qualities into the overall justification of the steady development of the human race in terms of wealth and moral well-being.

According to this metanarrative, the justification of science is related to wealth and education. The development of history is seen as a steady progress towards civilization or moral well-being. The language game of human passions, qualities and faults, is seen as steadily shifting in favour of our qualities and away from our faults as science and historical developments help us to conquer our faults in favour of our qualities. The point is that any event ought to be able to be understood in terms of the justifications of this meta-narrative; anything that happens can be understood and judged according to the discourse of human emancipation. For example, for any new social, political or scientific revolution we could ask the question 'Is this revolution a step towards the greater well-being of the mass of human beings?' It should always be possible to answer this question in terms of the rules of justification of the metanarrative of human emancipation.

Lyotard's linguistic law can be understood as stating that such metanarratives cannot justify what they claim to justify. In the words of *The Postmodern Condition*:

> In contemporary society and culture – postindustrial society, postmodern culture – the question of the legitimation of knowledge is formulated in different terms. The grand narrative has lost its credibility, regardless of what mode of unification it uses, regardless of whether it is a speculative narrative or a narrative of emancipation. (Lyotard 1984b: 37)

This means that the actual state of society necessarily involves competing language games, because there can be no unifying language game bringing all rules of legitimation into one. Lyotard calls this impossibility of metanarratives in the actual state of society 'delegitimation'. In a process of delegitimation, the classic meta-narratives of legitimation such as the discourse of human emancipation and the Marxist metanarrative have lost their ability to determine the legitimacy of all possible events. According to Lyotard, this process also holds true for the language game of science: instead of occupying the centre ground of society, as ultimate arbiter on matters of truth, science becomes just another game among many. Lyotard marks the delegitimation of science as one of the key moments of postmodernity. In the postmodern condition there is a loss of confidence in the ability of science to regulate questions in other domains: 'the road is then open for an important current of postmodernity: science plays its own game; it is incapable of legitimating the other games' (Lyotard 1984b: 40).

The necessary failure of unifying metanarratives brings about the multiplication of incommensurable language games. The two processes form a major part of Lyotard's description of the actual state of society, the matter at hand for philosophy:

> The social subject itself seems to dissolve in this dissemination of language games. The social bond is linguistic, but it is not woven with a single thread. It is a fabric formed by the intersection of at least two (and in reality an indeterminate number) of language games, obeying different rules. Wittgenstein writes: 'Our language can be seen as an ancient city: a maze of little streets and squares, of old and new houses with additions from recent periods; and this surrounded by a multitude of new boroughs with straight regular streets and uniform houses.' (1984b: 40)

So there is multiplicity of language games and this multiplicity can never be unified under a single metanarrative. This then allows for a deduction of the classic definition of the postmodern condition: a fragmented society with many different and incompatible moral and social codes.

It is one thing, though, to note the failure of certain metanarratives in the face of events, it is another to claim that they must *always* fail. Lyotard's description of the process of delegitimation in *The Postmodern Condition* cannot lead to the claim that unifying metanarratives can never justify all possible events. In order to rectify this lack, Lyotard restates his disbelief in metanarratives in terms of a universal law determined from within his philosophy of language but dependent, as will be shown below, on feelings and his understanding of events. The law can be called the law of concatenation, for it pertains to the linking of phrases. It states: 'To link is necessary, but how to link is not.'

This law is developed in *The Differend* in terms of the question of what is the just way of following on from a given phrase. Firstly, the following of one sentence with another is presented as unavoidable. Something happens and every act after the event is a response to it. This point shows the element of responsibility involved in following a phrase. We cannot evade the need to think through our response, the next phrase:

> 102. For there to be no phrase is impossible, for there to be *And a phrase* is necessary. It is necessary to make linkage. This is not an obligation, a

Sollen [an ought to], but a necessity, a *Müssen* [a must]. To link is necessary but how to link is not. (Lyotard 1988a: 66)

Secondly, the law states that there is no necessary, necessarily
just, way of following one phrase with another. There are just links
to be made but these will always be relative to a particular language
game or genre. Lyotard calls this relation one of 'pertinence' or
'suitability', where a link can only be judged as pertinent or suitable
from within a particular genre or language game: 'It is necessary to
link, but the mode of linking is never necessary. It is suitable or
unsuitable' (1988a: 29). This law is also stated, in a slightly different
form elsewhere in *The Differend*:

> 136. To link is necessary, but a particular linkage is not. This linkage can
> be declared pertinent, though, and the phrase that does the stating is a
> rule for linking. It is a constitutive part of a genre of discourse: after such
> and such a kind of phrase, here are the phrases that are permitted. (1988a:
> 80)

Thus Lyotard's disbelief in metanarratives has been put in the
form of a law. There are language games which have rules as to
what is a pertinent concatenation but there can be no overall language game whose rules for just concatenation apply to all cases.
Rather, any given phrase can be pertinently linked on to another in
many different ways according to different language games. There
is no rule to determine which is the just language game for any
given phrase. The existence of such a rule would allow a
metanarrative to be constituted: the metanarrative would corre-
spond to the language game to which the rule belonged. In order to
avoid this, Lyotard's law of concatenation states that there can be no
metanarratives because there can be no rule. This is the difference
between 'pertinent' or 'suitable', on the one hand, and 'necessary',
on the other; the former apply to the relative case of a specific
language game or genre, while the latter applies to all possible
language games. The law of concatenation is a further aspect of the
actual state of society or matter at hand. In this society or matter
there can be no universal rules as to what a just action could be;
there are only rules relative to particular language games or genres.
But how does Lyotard deduce his law of concatenation? Is this only
another form of belief or are there grounds for the law?

Once again, in order to answer these questions we must refer to
Lyotard's work on feelings and events. The law follows from the
fact that any phrase can be an event associated with the feeling of the

sublime. A phrase occurs, not as a link in a chain of phrases, but as an independent event. In the following quote, Lyotard defines the phrase as an event and also draws a parallel between a moment out of time, the now, and a phrase independent of a concatenation, the phrase event: 'As being what it is this time, the now is taken as occurrence, as an event. I would say, as a phrase event. There is *There is*, a phrase taken as an occurrence, as *what*, which rightly said is not the now, but now.' (Lyotard 1988a: 74). We come to know, or rather to feel that the phrase is independent of any concatenation through the feeling of the sublime associated with the occurrence of the phrase. Lyotard insists that the occurrence of a phrase is independent of any representation or understanding we may have of it. Instead, we feel the occurrence of the phrase; we feel it as a void that has been filled.

In the following important passage from *The Differend*, this point is made in parallel to comments about a moment outside time. The passage is interesting because it frames the event in the context of an ontology, a philosophy of being. In effect, in *The Differend* Lyotard extends his theme of the event to the study of being; to be is to be an event:

> The occurrence, the phrase, as a *what* that happens, does not at all stem from the question of time, but from that of Being/non-Being. This question is called forth by a feeling: it is possible for nothing to happen. Silence not as a phrase in abeyance, but as a non-phrase, a non *what*. This feeling is anxiety or surprise: there is something rather than nothing. Scarcely is this phrased, than the occurrence is chained, registered and forgotten in the occurrence of this phrase, which, in stating the *There is*, binds the occurrence by comparing it with its absence. (Lyotard 1988a: 75)

The feeling of anxiety mentioned here is essential because it conveys the disturbance associated with the occurrence of the phrase. The occurrence disturbs our conception of time as a succession of moments and it disturbs our conception of phrases as necessarily involved in specific concatenations. The feeling of anxiety indicates that something came out of nothing; in a sense the 'now' and the phrase owe nothing to time and to concatenations. This feeling of anxiety will be exploited by Lyotard in his study of the sublime as a balance to the pleasure and delight associated with the opportunity for concatenation presented by a new phrase (see chapter 5).

Once Lyotard has shown that phrases are events, he can apply the two properties he always ascribes to events to phrases. This allows him to draw two conclusions: first, that phrases are unique occurrences, they cannot be predicted; second, that phrases as events can never be fully represented or understood. However, any linking on from a phrase constitutes a partial understanding of it and fixes it in a particular language game. This fixing can never be legitimate because the phrase as event is beyond representation. From this remark Lyotard can deduce the law of concatenation: 'To link is necessary, but how to link is not.' Phrases are events; not only is it impossible to predict when they are going to occur, but also we cannot know for sure how to link other phrases on to them:

> 138. A linkage may reveal an equivocalness in the previous phrase. *The door is closed* can give rise to *Of course, what do you think doors are for?*, or to *I know, they're trying to lock me in*, or to *All the better, I have to talk to you*, etc. (1988a: 81)

It appears, then, that the best we can do is determine suitable or pertinent links according to given language games. But even this best is under constant threat because of the unpredictable occurrence of phrases associated with the sublime feeling. They make us feel the limits of any given language game and genre and thereby force us to seek a new genre to determine new suitable or pertinent links: 'The differend is the unstable state of language wherein something which must be able to be put into phrases cannot yet be' (1988a: 13). The postmodern condition is a discomforting state; it involves regions of apparent security, language games, and moments of great uncertainty, events or the conflicts of language games over phrase events. There is no absolute certainty here, only a constant threat to relative certainty through events and the feeling of the sublime.

4

States of Society: the Libidinal Economy

General features of the libidinal economy

'Work as the sun does when you're sunbathing or taking grass' (Lyotard 1993a: 1). Lyotard's libidinal philosophy shares the rebelliousness of the sixties. It attempts to break with traditions on the level of ideas, method and style. Accordingly, *Libidinal Economy* is a shocking and off-beat book in terms of content and writing. It is unusual to encounter a humorous mix of sexual desire, gut reactions and technical terms from myriad fields in a work of philosophy: 'We abhor therapeutics and its vaseline, we prefer to burst under the quantitative excesses that you judge the most stupid. And don't wait for our spontaneity to rise up in revolt either' (1993a: 116). The book experiments with practical desires and avoids abstract ideas and ideals. It shows no obvious signs of a search for truth and logical consistency. Desires are expressed in as direct way as possible: they are enacted rather than represented. That is, they are designed to be felt rather than understood. If one lazily seeks to detect a clearly expressed theory and philosophical position in *Libidinal Economy*, Lyotard's rebellion makes the philosophy confusing to the point of disgust. On the other hand, it can also allow for an exciting, if equally difficult, escape from a dominant approach to theoretical writing. *Libidinal Economy* can attract readers through their senses and feelings, through scraps of knowledge or through oblique references. It can do so without having to expect that they have been trained in, or seek, a particular approach to truth or theory.

Lyotard describes both types of difficulty in the last sections of

Libidinal Economy. He is explicit in refusing traditional modes of theory and styles of writing. In particular, he writes against theory as a static and detached discourse that attempts to tell the truth about a topic. Instead, *Libidinal Economy* is an attempt to release desire by showing it at work. The static aspect of theory is its consistency, the way in which terms are repeated reliably on the basis of a clear and well-defined or distinct definition. The detached aspect is the distance theory draws between itself and its topic. Though the topic may be an emotion or a desire, a thing in confused and complex movement, the theory about it remains clear and immobile. Libidinal philosophy, on the other hand, must not be distinguished from desire or emotions, from any of its topics. On the contrary, it seeks to release and to channel those very things that theory seeks to keep at a distance. Reliable repetition of abstract, clear and well-defined terms is not its business.

Does this mean that it is futile to approach the work in terms of truth and in terms of meaning? Does it mean that one must either be drawn to the book immediately, or be dismissed as a 'theorist' or someone with the 'wrong desires'? Does it mean that any attempt to introduce the work is inconsistent or impossible within the project of a libidinal philosophy? No. Though particular views of theory and philosophy, clarity and truth are rejected by Lyotard, it is still possible to follow clearly specific aspects of his libidinal work. Lyotard puts forward arguments, deploys original concepts and builds up a recognizable philosophy or world-view. He does so even at the very moment when he attacks the cold detachment of theory. The attack depends on the argument that theory is not as cold and pure as it may seem. Coldness and immobility can be interpreted as desire for the immobilization of the prey and for the exact repetition of methods and terms. In this sense, theory can be viewed as a libidinal practice, driven by a very specific desire, something like voyeurism or sadism.

This reading of a topic in terms of desire is typical. There is a consistent practice and associated terminology running through *Libidinal Economy*. Matter is always treated in terms of desire, in terms of libido, even if that treatment is itself libidinal or highly charged. So it is possible to approach Lyotard's work in terms of a relatively reliable philosophy: a philosophy of the economy of desire. Though, given Lyotard's move away from abstract theory, this approach has to begin with specific practical cases, such as his attack on theory outlined above. The point of the approach will be, firstly, to seek to understand what general claims are presupposed about

existence and society in practical cases. Secondly, it will be to understand how these claims lead to new forms of political, philosophical
and artistic action. Finally, it is possible to enquire into the basis for
Lyotard's claims and into the validity of his deduction of new forms
of action.

Thus Lyotard's definition of society as libidinal economy is an
attempt to emphasize the role of desire in the functioning of society.
Desire is understood as a material process that involves systems and
energy (the system of repetition and distance and the energy pent
up by them in theory or sexual practices, for instance). The libidinal
economy is a flow of resources around a system where resources
take the form of an energy that circulates and appears in many
different, ever changing subsystems. The energy takes the form of
libidinal feelings and desires (Lyotard calls these intensities). The
use of libidinal here indicates an expansion of the model of sexual
desire and feelings into a general model for energy in society: energy in the libidinal economy is like sexual energy. This energy is
highly unstable. That is, libidinal intensities – feelings and desires –
emerge in an unpredictable manner. What is more, although the
economy exploits intensities, it never fully understands or controls
them. Lyotard attaches great importance to the sexual and psycho-
analytic connotations introduced through the term libidinal: the
relation between the economy and intensities is as unpredictable as
the relation between our actions in everyday life and the workings
of the unconscious. Thus the libidinal economy is a system driven
by the energy of desire.

After intensities, the most important – and most puzzling – aspect
of the libidinal economy is the space where intensities first occur:
Lyotard calls it the libidinal band. This space is known only as the
place where feelings and desires occur; beyond that, it is ill-defined.
The libidinal band knows no boundaries and has no recognizable
stable features, other than its critical role as the place where the
energy in the economy meets the structures that exploit it. This role
is all-important because it allows Lyotard to maintain rigid systems
for the exploitation of energy or unpredictable intensities without
having to explain one in terms of the other; they both go through a
transition stage on the libidinal band. Once feelings and desires
have appeared in the economy, they are given recognizable shape
by the way they are handled by various structures or set-ups; Lyotard
calls these dispositions and figures. These figures and dispositions
channel, control and exploit the energy of intensities. For example, it
could be said that the nuclear family is a disposition controlling and

exploiting desires and feelings called lust, love, affection and so on. However, in the same way as the desire that is exploited by the disposition of the nuclear family can also destroy it, through adultery for example, all dispositions are at risk from new unpredictable and unmanageable intensities.

It is possible to see the libidinal economy as an imaginary planet in flux. At the core of the planet, there is an incandescent mass, prone to shock waves and sudden changes in temperature. These changes are driven by unpredictable forces way beyond our understanding of the laws that govern the mass proper. The forces are equivalent to libidinal intensities; the mass is the libidinal band. Like the band, the mass is a transition stage between the forces and the more rigid outer layer of the planet. This layer is made up of a series of moving plates whose movements make and unmake further plates. The plates consist of cooling matter from the core mass and their movements are linked to the temperature and flows of the mass. These plates are the structures that channel the energy behind the mass into continents; they are equivalent to dispositions. As a whole, this planet is similar to Lyotard's libidinal economy; imagine our society as the development of living structures on the plates.

So the libidinal economy is an unstable actual state of society. New flows of energy constantly challenge established ways of handling energy and this constant appearance of new intensities alters the boundaries and operation of specific dispositions. However, it is not only the appearance of the new that challenges set-ups or dispositions: the exploited intensities also attack the disposition from within. This is because any disposition operates with a false understanding and representation of the energies it exploits. Imagine a breed of brilliant scientists on the surface of the planet mentioned above. These scientists, having studied the flows of the core mass, recommend the positioning of towns so as to exploit the heat of the core as safely as possible. Unfortunately, but inevitably – intensities cannot be fully predicted or understood – the scientists are mistaken. Their kind disappears in a flow of molten rock. An extremely stupid and superstitious band of cold cave dwellers, on the other hand, survives and flourishes. Feelings and desires cannot be understood or represented by dispositions; this means that any disposition is at risk from the intensities it has trapped and misrepresents. An example of this could be the way the feeling of love exploited by the nuclear family can give way to destructive feelings of jealousy, as members of the family seek ever greater degrees of love and freedom. This also means that no given rationalization or valuation of feelings and desires is valid outside the boundaries of a limited field. In the case of the scientists and the rock dwellers, the judgement as to the greater stupidity of the latter turns out to be false if intelligence is judged in terms of survival.

The impossibility of a proper understanding or use of intensities means that there can be many different figures and dispositions exploiting intensities. None of these dispositions fully understands or controls the feelings and desires whose energy it exploits. Thus the libidinal economy is a state of society where many different set-ups offer conflicting ways of controlling feelings and desires. In addition to this, dispositions themselves set off intensities, that is, the structures channelling energy are themselves energy sources. For instance, the movement of the unfortunate scientists on the surface of the planet can give rise to new forces at the core. In fact, they could have been responsible for their own downfall. The worst-case scenario of global warming is a good example of this unpredictable cycle: a given structure, capitalist economies bent on ever-increasing consumption, give rise to catastrophic flooding that brings down those economies, while new structures emerge to exploit the new energy sources. These new structures need not be human; indeed, Lyotard's account does not allow for a privileging of the human form above all others. It must be stressed, though, that according to Lyotard this chain of events cannot be fully predicted as to its outcome. It is possible to act in such a way as to encourage or discourage the emergence of intensities within a disposition, but which intensities will emerge and which structures will then seek to exploit them is unpredictable.

Dispositions deny the unpredictability of intensities, because exploitation demands some degree of predictability. However, certain dispositions go so far as to involve general claims about all feelings and all desires. Not only do they attempt to control intensities in a specific situation, but they claim to understand the proper way for all dispositions to exploit all feelings. Religious and political-economical dispositions can be of this type. For instance, Lyotard notes how Christian religions have attempted to extend their dominion over all dispositions, the family, the state, sexuality, education, even business, and over all possible feelings and desires – through the concept of sin, for instance. It is possible to find similar dispositions in a Marxist or Hegelian political economy, but also in the operation of capitalist societies where the market and the laws of the market serve to control and exploit the emergence of any intensity. The libidinal economy involves all sorts of dispositions, from overarching ones such as a capitalist economy, to small and detailed ones such as a specific sexual practice, sado-masochism for instance. Lyotard's description of the libidinal economy is aimed at the definition of political acts while taking account of the emergence and exploitation of intensities and of the many dispositions involved in that exploitation.

The event in a libidinal context

The last few lines of *Libidinal Economy* are a political affirmation of desire and intensities. Libidinal politics allows energy to emerge in the form of libidinal intensities, feelings and desires: 'What would be interesting would be to stay put, but quietly seize every chance to function as good intensity-conducting bodies.' Like phrases in the later philosophy, libidinal intensities are events, their occurrence cannot be predicted, yet it grabs our attention or it is our attention: 'In sum, there are events: something happens which is not tautological with what has happened' (Lyotard 1988a: 79). This property of exceeding or going beyond the powers of representation is given as an essential factor in *Discours, figure*, Lyotard's theoretical book that can be seen as the groundwork for *Libidinal Economy*, the main book of his philosophy of the libidinal economy: 'The event as disturbance always defies knowledge; it can defy knowledge articulated as discourse; but it can also shake the body in its own quasi-understandin̪ᵤ, as in emotion, rendering it out of touch with itself and other things' (Lyotard 1971: 22).

As Lyotard puts it later, in *Libidinal Economy*, the event happens on a body and the body is changed by that happening. But once the event is recorded in words or on a body, through a reaction or a practice for example, then some aspect of it has been lost:

> And all the comparisons which may come to mind, they are damned in advance by the accumulation (*cum*) which they comprise and which subject them to procedures of weighing, thought, commensurability, good for the register and accountability, for ever incapable of yielding intensity in its *event*. (Lyotard 1993a: 18)

In *Libidinal Economy*, Lyotard develops the theoretical terms 'incompossibility', 'figure' and 'disposition' in order to describe the consequences of that occurrence. The occurrence of intensities gives rise to a space called the libidinal band. This occurrence then gives rise to figures and dispositions, that is, recognizable forms and set-ups. Feelings such as an overwhelming pain, a 'suffering through excess', lead to the existence of different and incompatible figures and set-ups or dispositions in one place; for example, the set-up of stress associated with pressure at work and the figure of a blood clot on the brain are both accounts of a certain pain. This place is the space in which intensities (feelings and desires) occur; it is called the libidinal band or libidinal skin.

The libidinal band is like a body, but unlike the body the libidinal band does not have set organic parts: it is made up of the aftermath of the passage of feelings and desires rather than made of parts in which desires occur. This difficult definition of a space as the trail or aftermath of intensities is a result of the unpredictable and disturbing aspects of events. We cannot know the space where events occur because this would lead to the possibility of knowing when and how they occur. For example, if feelings occurred on the body and doctors knew the body extremely well, then it would be possible to explain, understand and predict the occurrence of these feelings. They would then no longer be events in Lyotard's sense. To avoid the problem he uses the difficult definition of a new space that we are not familiar with; this space cannot be known except as an aftermath of events and as the space where events can occur.

Narrative and libidinal economy

Lyotard explains these difficult libidinal economical terms best in his article 'Petite économie libidinale d'un dispositif narratif: la régie Renault raconte le meurtre de Pierre Overney', from the collection of essays that use and develop the description of the libidinal economy, *Des Dispositifs pulsionnels* (Lyotard 1980a). In the article, Lyotard studies the account of the murder of a demonstrator outside the Renault factory at Billancourt. This account, handed to the press by the Renault management, is an attempt to limit the damage to the firm of the event of the murder of Overney. Lyotard shows how the murder is an event in his sense. He also shows how the Renault account limits its intensity, suppresses the feelings and desires that accompany it, by fitting the event into a narrative, that is, a disposition or set-up. Note how in this use of disposition the term means an arrangement or set-up and not a state of a person disposed to do something. Narrative and theatricality militate against intensity; instead of releasing desire they bind it or repress it through attempts to control and exploit it. In turn, this repression and the power necessary to achieve it depend on the logic of reference and lack. The narrative and theatre set up a scene removed from an original event and controlled by those in charge of narration (in this case, the Renault management). The attack on this logic is therefore, at the same time, an attack on the power of narrative and theatricality and on those who seek to exploit such power at the expense of intensity.

Lyotard's point is that there can be no set-up that can truly account for the event, not even the account of the damage to Overney's body or the emotional figure of the dying demonstrator. Rather, the event gives rise to the body and all the other set-ups, but none of these can ever be 'true to the event' – although some may limit the intensity of the event more than others. Dispositions and figures are produced, events occur:

> If Overney's death is an event it is not *on that body*, on the contrary, the body will have to be (re)produced from the death, as an instantaneous tension that cannot be localized in an n-dimensional libidinal space-time. If there is a *body* corresponding to such a space-time, it is certainly not the organic body . . . (Lyotard 1980a: 178)

The difficult terminology here is a result of Lyotard's need to describe a space that does not enforce limits on the occurrence of events, an ill-defined space that knows no internal limits and no external limits, that does not involve partitions, sections and so on:

> This body knows no limits. It does not stop at a surface or frontier (the skin) that would dissociate an interior and an exterior. The body is extended easily beyond that so-called frontier because words, books, food, images, glances, pieces of body, animals, sounds and gestures can be invested in. Therefore they can function as charged regions and as outflow canals, in the same way as an 'organ' such as the liver or stomach in psychosomatic emotions or illnesses. (Lyotard 1980a: 179)

The Overney article is Lyotard's attempt to think through an event and in so doing he has realized that any account of the death is political. There is no true account of this event, only different set-ups designed to increase or decrease, control and divert the flows of intensities. The strength of his thinking is in the realization that this politicization of accounts depends on a difficult and paradoxical philosophy of events. Had Lyotard succumbed to the temptation of selecting a well-defined space for the occurrence of events, then he would have produced a space for non-political true accounts: 'The organic body is a political body, in the current sense of political economy. It is given limits circumscribing its *property* of body proper; a regimen or an administration is assigned to it and this is its constitutional system' (1980a: 179).

This ill-defined space, the libidinal band, does not have the limits and borders of the body. This explains the bizarre, yet exciting and liberating, opening of *Libidinal Economy*, 'Open the so-called body and spread out all its surfaces . . .' The opening is an attempt to draw parallels with the body but with none of its delimitations. In fact there is a release of energy as the imposition of the human form is lifted to reveal the libidinal band. In this sense, 'we' are the libidinal band and that is all. Lyotard's description of the libidinal band as a Moebius strip can also be understood along these lines. Once the body has been opened up to form a strip, the two ends are joined up with a single twist. This turns the libidinal strip into a Moebius band, that is a one-sided infinite loop. The Moebius strip therefore allows him to reduce the number of delimitations on the libidinal space. Defined as a Moebius strip, the libidinal band no longer has a beginning, an end, or two different sides. Lyotard can claim that such a thing as the libidinal band exists because it is the crossing point of feelings, figures and dispositions:

> The libidinal thing is a kind of band with one infinite surface (a Moebius strip) and, at the same time, it is a sort of labyrinth, a surface covered in nooks and crannies, undecidable connections for thousands of routes over which pass intensity potentials. (Lyotard 1980a: 179)

The concept of labyrinth mentioned in the quote above is important to Lyotard. The labyrinth is made up of all the changing figures and set-ups or dispositions that come to account for and control intensities, feelings and desires as events. Later, in *Libidinal Economy*, Lyotard uses the labyrinth as a way of describing a single disposition in which desires and feelings are trapped. With nowhere to go they circulate in desperation, until, 'with a scream', another feeling, affect or desire emerges on the surface of the libidinal band. The scream that goes with a sudden crack-up marks the shift from one disposition to another. A crisis has occurred in one system through the emergence of an intensity that it cannot handle. A new system will have to be built to contain it. For example, a *coup de foudre* or eruption of passion leads us to break with a settled, well-organized life. It indicates an insufficiency or deficiency in that organization. So plans are made for a new one that will 'preserve' and 'secure' the new passion. Desire is satisfied in it in many different and more or less satisfactory ways. These structural preparations and after-effects of the initial eruption are the labyrinth. They capture the initial feeling and bend it to a particular pattern. However, according to Lyotard's philosophy, the feeling or drive will never be at home in the labyrinth: sooner or later a scream will indicate the forlorn status of the attempt to tame the feeling.

A specific place on the band can be described by referring to the changes in the set-ups and figures at that place. However, it is important to remember that any such description is provisional and incomplete. It cannot recapture the initial events that gave rise to a particular labyrinth, neither can it predict how and when new events will disturb it again. The libidinal band changes when new feelings and desires occur. Dispositions and figures take their place on the libidinal band in the aftermath of the emergence of intensities; in fact, they testify to the passage of intensities:

> Therefore not a surface first, then a writing or inscription over it. But the libidinal skin of which *after the event*, one will be able to say that it is made up of a patchwork of organs, of elements from organic and social bodies, the libidinal skin initially like the *track* of intensities, ephemeral work, useless like a jet trail in the thin air at an altitude of 10,000 . . . (Lyotard 1993a: 17)

Figures and dispositions are the ways in which an intensity gives rise to shapes, to labyrinths, on the libidinal band – in the same way as a feeling or desire gives rise to a form or an account. For example, pain can shape the face in a certain way and Lyotard speaks of the figure as a mask. The intensity, the feeling or desire, gives rise to a shape or a mask, it defines the limits of an organ or region of the body. This definition is produced on the libidinal band as intensities are followed by the crossing of figures or dispositions: 'In fact this organic body is the ceaseless product – product which must be constantly produced – of operations, manipulations, ablations, diaereses, grafts, occlusions and derivations on the labyrinthine libidinal band' (Lyotard 1980a: 179).

A good way of understanding this process is the image of the patterns and shapes produced on a mirror after a hammer blow. The hammer blow is the event. The patterns are the set-ups and figures that come after the event as evidence for its occurrence. Any part of the libidinal band is like a mirror that has been hit and is being hit many times in different places. It is in this way that intensities allow various accounts to be formulated and associated. The desire associated with a figure on the body, the ear lobe or the fold at the knee, for example, gives rise to the figure and to the various accounts we associate with it. Accounts, understandings and interpretations of the intensity will then be possible through the medium of the figure or the disposition, because they can be repeated and represented in a structural and hence in a linguistic account:

> First, that means that there is no notable difference between a libidinal formation and a discursive formation, in so far as they are both formations, *Gestaltungen*. A libidinal *dispositif*, considered precisely, as a stabilization and even a stasis or group of energetic stases, is, examined formally, a structure. Conversely, what is essential to a structure, when it is approached in economic terms, is that its fixity or consistency, which allows spatio-temporal maintenance of identical denominations between a this and a not-this, work on a pulsionnal movement as would dams, sluices and channels. (Lyotard 1993a: 25)

In this crucial passage from *Libidinal Economy*, we see the libidinal economy take shape. It is an economy that involves intensities (pulsions) and the dispositions set up to regulate them. The dispositions control feelings and desires, for example they give accounts of the 'proper' use of a feeling or of the 'proper' way to exploit and satisfy desires. But the feelings also have a hold over the dispositions, that is, the occurrence of feelings and desires can challenge any given disposition and thereby demand a new set-up.

Figures and dispositions are linked through the event in the same way as the various patterns on a mirror lead back to the point of impact of the hammer blow. But, unlike the supposedly clear chain of cause and effect at work on the mirror, the different set-ups and figures cannot be brought together through the medium of the event. This is because none of them can be said to lead back accurately and truthfully to it. Lyotard concludes that intensities can give rise to incompossible figures, figures that do not seem to be possible together, a mask of pleasure and a mask of pain, for instance: '[The suffering] proceeds from the *incompossibility* of figures, of masks which together occupy the same space-time and thereby reveal the libidinal band' (1993a: 11). Incompossible figures occupy the same place on the libidinal band because an intensity can give rise to a variety of different figures. So an intensity occurs, a disposition or figure then channels it into a given structure, but this does not stop another figure or disposition from following the intensity and channelling it into another structure. Intensities give rise to incompossible figures and dispositions on the libidinal band. Different understandings, interpretations and ways of managing or accounting for an event are brought together, but cannot be compared or measured through the medium of the event. Thus the murder of Overney, for example, brings the account of the bosses and the account of the militant demonstrators together, but these accounts cannot be measured according to the real event, what really happened. That event has gone never to be recaptured; all we are left with are incompossible accounts – accounts that deny each other as possibilities.

However, although single figures or dispositions cannot be said to have an accurate hold on the intensities they channel, intensities can be associated with the meeting of incompossible figures or dispositions. According to Lyotard, the emergence of an intense feeling or desire shows that two apparently incompatible and inconsistent accounts have found themselves to be in one place. For example, desire shows how the incompossible dispositions of hearing and sexual foreplay have met at the point of the ear lobe: the organ associated with hearing has also become a sexual orifice. The image Lyotard uses to express this association of pain, pleasure and incompossible figures is that of the different accounts of sex in the loss of virginity. There the figure of virginity encounters the figure of desire. In *Libidinal Economy*, this encounter is given through the pagan gods said to preside over the sexual act. Lyotard wishes to argue, against Saint Augustine's argument in favour of one God, that the incompatible gods of virginity and loss of virginity are the only way to explain the cry forced out during the encounter:

> Virginensis [the god who strips the girdle from the young girl] is a cry
> forced out by all this at once, a cry made of several incompossible cries:
> she opens up, he takes me, she resists, he squeezes, she gets loose, he
> starts and stops, she obeys and commands, this could happen, happen
> impossibly. (Lyotard 1993a: 8)

There is not the one Christian God but many, pagan, gods present at this act; only this can explain the cries. The matter at hand, which Lyotard calls the libidinal band here, is occupied by incompossible figures. Intense cries of pleasure and pain indicate this incompossibility; according to Lyotard, the Christian account of the loss of virginity cannot account for those cries and hence denies incompossibility:

> This suffering through excess is that of the Bacchants, it proceeds from
> the *incompossibility* of figures, of masks which together occupy the
> same space-time and thereby reveal the libidinal band; for such an

incompossibility where several parts, however different, of the alleged organic body, are affirmed at the same time, or even, if you prefer, where sections of the psychic and social apparatus which must only be affirmed separately or successively, are affirmed at the same time; it is unbearable. (1993a: 11)

Lyotard and Freud

Lyotard's dependence on the libidinal can seem odd in a philosophy book with a specifically political calling. This apparent peculiarity is resolved when we realize that he is attempting to explain the paradoxical relation between feelings, affects and desires and the figures and dispositions at the basis of any account of those intensities. Sexual and psychological examples and theories provide an excellent support for the general lessons he wants to draw from the relations of events to accounts of events. However, to understand the importance of this reference to sexuality and the unconscious, it is useful to return to Lyotard's careful yet ground-breaking reading of Freud, first developed in *Discours, figure*, then pursued and altered in *Dérive à partir de Marx et Freud* and *Libidinal Economy*.

In *Discours, figure*, Lyotard borrows from Freud's study of the unconscious in order to explain the relation of figure to discourse through the relation of consciousness and the unconscious. In particular, Lyotard concentrates on Freud's work on denial (see 'Le non et la position de l'objet' to 'Freud: la (dé)negation', in 1971: 116–34) to give an account of negation which goes beyond grammatical, logical and structural formulations. For this account alone, the work stands as one of the most thorough critical reactions to structuralism in its relation to discourse and to aesthetics. Lyotard deploys his deep knowledge of art and psychoanalysis to go beyond structuralist theory and accounts of meaning. The aim is to show how forms of discursive negation indicate an essential role for desire in discourse. This role cannot be fully represented from within the discourse desire operates on.

These points develop into important criticisms of structuralism and into facets essential to any theory of meaning that goes beyond it. First, the structuralist dependence on a fundamental logic of negation and on oppositions between terms in language must hide deeper relations. Second, these relations must be thought of in terms of desire. Lyotard looks at denial as a case of negation in discourse. According to him, denial cannot be explained in terms of the logical negation of a proposition, since what is denied is also the object of a positive proposition which can be uncovered by the analyst. The structural distinction between signifiers within a system breaks down when a term is at the same time on both sides of a distinction, at the same time 'mother' and 'not mother'. The complexity of this simultaneity is rendered and explained by Freud, as interpreted by Lyotard, in terms of the different planes occupied by the desire for the mother, the destructive drive to negate while 'reconstituting' the negated object, and the plane of knowledge in discourse:

> In *denying* [*en se défendant*] having dreamed of his mother, in effect, the patient proceeds with the constitution or reconstitution of his mother as a 'lost object' and of what he says as discourse; he moves out of the plane of the dream and desire in order to occupy the plane of knowledge. Through the distanciation that is assumed prior to all discourse and all objectivity, through the rupture of the original identification, the patient institutes, once more, the order of language, and the order objectivity to which it refers, that is, the mother. (1971: 123)

What is crucial for Lyotard's argument in *Discours, figure*, but also in his later work on language and desire, and on intensity and dispositions, is that the interference between planes shows that an original split is the condition for constant disturbances within discourse and dispositions. These are instigated by the re-emergence of desire and intensity:

> In returning to these Freudian themes, we only treat part of the problem. Since the supposed split of the pre-world does not only open the distance wherein the eye will settle on the edge of discourse. That tearing produces effects of distortion *in* discourse. A figure, operating as the matrix of these effects, is settled deep in our speech; it takes on our words in order to make forms and images of them. The extent of desire makes a bed for our thoughts and beds them there. (1971: 129)

When Freud analyses a statement such as 'It is not my mother' and sums up with a paradoxical 'We therefore conclude that it is the mother', Lyotard sees that the analyst has gone beyond the simple logical negation where there cannot be at the same time an affirmation 'It is my mother' and negation 'It is not my mother.' Further, he sees that there must also be a surpassing of the structuralist understanding of negation as being dependent on a system of opposition or discontinuities. There has to be a way of explaining the simultaneous affirmation and denial of the reference to the mother in language. Thus, in his observations on denial, Freud has opened up a way for Lyotard to introduce the affirmative desire (for the mother) into discourse, and as a condition for discourse: 'Syntactical negation, structural negative, intentional negativity. Is it possible, certainly not to reduce them to one another, but to articulate them?' (1971: 121). The reference to the mother, any reference, involves the discursive setting up of a system of opposition, the logical possibility of negation, *and* the play of desire within language. What the process of denial shows is that reference to an object from within a discursive set-up has the potential to be distorted by the operations of desire, 'the production of effects of distortion *in* discourse'.

The drive to knowledge and the drive to represent are therefore necessarily implicated in a process which at the same time explains their constant renewal and involves their failure as inherently stable set-ups or dispositions (to use the terminology of *Libidinal Economy*). To want to know, to give account, to tell a story is always to be driven by desire and to be governed by the operations of desire. Neither of which, according to Lyotard, can be captured in a metadiscourse on desire. Thus the unpredictable flows of energy on the libidinal band, and the position of intensities beyond knowledge and other dispositions (but as their condition, as in the case of denial) can be traced back to Lyotard's work on Freud in *Discours, figure*.

In the following passage, Lyotard deduces the emptiness (or perhaps more accurately, the nothingness) which separates speech and what it refers to, from the identification of the will to knowledge and the desire for knowledge. Freuds analyses the movement of the eye to the mother's breast and deduces an original schism that comes to divide the two. This schism is repeated in any desire for an object represented in speech:

> All objectivity will be inscribed in a distance opened up by a loss. Perception assumes this separation, which will serve as a model for a theory of knowledge. . . . We have to pose the identity of wanting to know and to desire . . . The will to know is implicated within discourse: turning *around* its object, in deep space, the object always concealing one of its faces. . . . The split [*Entzweiung*] places an unbridgeable gap *on the edge* of discourse. An edge of emptiness. Which means that when we speak we are not what we speak of, and that our speech awaits its respondent (its reference), on the other side, as is our desire. (Lyotard 1971: 128–9)

So the event of intensity, which leaves any disposition 'on hold', can be explained as a case of Freud's original split. Any reference presupposes this split and any knowledge, any desire for knowledge attempts the impossible, that is, to bridge the gap which is the condition of the desire.

However, already in *Discours, figure* (and all the more in *Dérive à partir de Marx et Freud* and *Libidinal Economy*), Lyotard has to go a step further than Freud; he has to be more radical with the split. The metadiscourse of analysis is itself to be attacked for its attempts to bridge the unbridgeable, to repair the original split. For example, in the essay 'Sur une figure de discours' in *Des Dispositifs pulsionnels*, Lyotard studies the 'dispositive at work in the psychoanalytical cure' in order to bring out its status as a machinery which 'captures, canalizes and disposes of libidinal energy'. The study is important because it makes a distinction between Freud's contribution to the concepts of libidinal economy, as shown in the work in *Discours, figure*, and the *political* economy at work in the talking cure of psychoanalysis:

> The movement of curing is from the incommunicable to the communicable, from the unexchangeable to the exchangeable ... The point is to capture and divert 'blocked' energy (or so it is claimed) into *scenes*, towards language. Thus it is to pass from libidinal economy to 'political' economy, to achieve the liquidation of high–low intensities through their reabsorption into language. We pass from spending to saving. (Lyotard 1980a: 140)

For Lyotard, this management of intensity in the disposition of psychoanalysis goes counter to the more radical understanding of the split between the intensities of the libidinal economy and the dispositions of political economy. There can be no legitimate disposition which could ever claim to represent flows of intensity. Any such representation, whether it went under the name of talking cure or any other name, would always deny the status of intensities as events. This channelling of the energy of intensities would therefore always be doomed, in the sense of always overtaken by new intensities and in the sense of always working against the energy it seeks to exploit.

The disposition of psychoanalysis is not positive in its status as cure but rather in its capacity to release new intensities. It does this through the creation of novel figures such as the unexchangeability of the I/Thou positions of the analyst and the patient: 'What is positive in that figure is the production of new libidinal operators, rather than "effects of sense" which must always be relative to the exteriority chosen to describe the disposition.' This is a return to the split described above, rather than to an effort to mend or resolve it.

In short, in Lyotard's reading of Freud, the value of psychoanalysis is as a disposition of torsion, that is, as a disposition that 'twists' narratives and discourse by insisting on the split between what is said and how it is interpreted. For example, in the relation of patient to analyst, or patient to dream, respective accounts twist what has occurred:

> That torsion is, so to speak, the emblem of pleasure [*jouissance*] in the disposition, the trace of a drift of pulsion, of death-pleasure. In my description of the discourse of faith or psychoanalysis, this torsion is localized in the *unexchangeability* of the positions *I/ Thou*. (1980a: 145)

This same drift comes to mark Lyotard's readings of Freud and Marx, as testified in his work *Dérive à partir de Marx et Freud* and even more so in *Libidinal Economy*. His discourse shares the same intensities and some of the same dispositions as theirs. But these are twisted into novel forms that are no longer consistent with the original. It is important, though, not to underestimate what Lyotard owes to the two 'old men'. This debt to Freud reappears in Lyotard's later philosophy, where he develops an interpretation of Freudian *Nachträgligkeit* and anamnesis in the context of the Kantian sublime. In *Heidegger et 'les juifs'* (1988), *Nachträgligkeit*, the re-enactment of an original shock in later feelings of fear and anguish (in the case of a phobia, for example), is analogous to the role played by the feeling of the sublime in communicating an event beyond understanding.

Incompossibility and the 'orienting zero'

The unpredictable occurrence of feelings and desires, of intensities, means that it is always possible for the libidinal band to alter. Furthermore, the occurrence of the intense feeling accompanies a conjunction of incompossible figures, that is, figures that involve a denial of each other's existence. Lyotard uses the term incompossible to express how absolute difference can occur beyond any reference to a reality or real world wherein all things would be related. He argues that intensities bring into light radical contradictions be-tween dispositions and figures on the libidinal band: therefore these cannot coexist and intense feelings are the signs of that impossibil-ity. Furthermore, there is no way of resolving this incompossibility born of intensities. In Lyotard's words there is no 'orientating zero', no scale to which both figures can be referred. It is impossible to think both figures together – their conjunction is only felt and then left as a trail on the libidinal band: 'The pain of incompossibility does not refer to a delimiting, selective, orientating zero. Thought does not precede it. More often than not, what is called thought is what escapes it, is produced as a way out of it' (Lyotard 1993a: 14). This limitation of the power of thought is what guarantees the absolute boundaries between figures as the pain erupts on the libidinal band.

The concept of the orienting zero detaches Lyotard's treatment of incompossibility from its origins in Leibniz's philosophy. This is made clear by Iain Hamilton Grant in his extremely helpful glossary to *Libidinal Economy*:

> 'compossibility' is a term used by Leibniz to indicate the relations between 'possible worlds'; many worlds are possible, but not possible together, not *compossible*. It is left to God, therefore, to create the 'best of all possible worlds', which, since He is perfect, He cannot fail to do. (in Lyotard 1993a: x)

For Leibniz, the perfection of God provides a principle for the selection and connection of possible worlds. Only the best of all possible worlds can have the greatest perfection of existing. But for Lyotard the orienting zero, 'the great Zero', does not come before all things, but after intensities. It cannot provide an ultimate principle for connecting worlds or dispositions, since it is only a factor of them: 'The great Zero is thus an empty centre which reduces the present complexity of what happens instantaneously on the band to a chamber of presence and absence' (Grant in Lyotard 1993a: xiii).

This does not mean that thought cannot try to reconcile both figures, cannot attempt a common understanding of them. Thought involves frameworks or dispositions whose whole purpose is to account for the occurrence of feelings and the apparent incompossibility of figures and other dispositions. Lyotard's point is that such an understanding will never be complete. The libidinal band is where the figures of our understanding come into contact with our feelings in an incomprehensible event. The figures and dispositions, though, can never fully account for the event because the occurrence of the intense feeling brings to light absolute differences between figures and between dispositions. This absolute difference is a barrier to forms of thought aimed at resolving differences and at explaining events.

Lyotard's philosophy is an attack on such forms. His critical reaction to the interpretation of the event as 'tragic' or 'repressed' or 'ambivalent' or 'castrated' can be explained along these lines. To claim that the event is in some way tragic or repressed or castrated is always to make impossible claims about the nature of events. Thus, according to Lyotard, events cannot be understood in the light of some great measure or master plan, the Will of God, for example. Again, he calls these references to some outside force or will that explains the occurrence of events, but that cannot itself be understood, references to the great Zero. It is not because we cannot fully understand a force behind intensities that they do not fit into one or another disposition. It is not because our understanding is castrated. It is because intensities have that property in themselves: 'And every intensity, scorching or remote, is always *this and not-this*, not at all through the effect of castration, of repression, of ambivalence, of tragedy due to the great Zero' (1993a: 15).

The strange and apparently evasive description of the libidinal band comes about in *Libidinal Economy* through Lyotard's attempt to explain that intensities are beyond understanding in themselves. He has to explain how feelings and desires can occur unpredictably and how that occurrence is associated with absolutely different figures or accounts of the feeling. Had Lyotard stuck with a more traditional concept he could not have explained the unpredictability or the difference. This is because such a concept – the body, for example – is already the result of a single unifying account, where it is possible to explain the occurrence of feelings and reconcile or judge opposing understandings of that occurrence. Lyotard does not accept that such traditional concepts really account for what our existence is really like. Intense feelings can only occur on something like the libidinal band. For Lyotard, the body and other traditional concepts are necessarily inadequate frameworks (figures and dispositions) for the understanding of processes on the libidinal band because they themselves are the result of such processes:

> everything that gives itself as object (thing, picture, text, body . . .) is *produced*, that is, it is the result of the metamorphosis of energy from a form into others. Every object is energy *at rest*, quiescent, provisionally *conserved, inscribed*. The disposition or figure is only a *metamorphic operator*. It is *itself* stabilized, conserved energy. Freud uses the word *investment* in this (more military than financial) sense. (1980a: 132)

Lyotard and Marx

Libidinal Economy seeks to distinguish itself from Marxist political economy. It is important to stress, though, that this distinction does not involve drawing a line between libidinal economy and Marxist political economy, but working to subvert and exploit Marx from within. The interest in subversion comes from the close relation of libidinal economy to Marxist political economy. Lyotard's early work for *Socialisme ou Barbarie* and *Pouvoir Ouvrier*, on Algeria, was within the Marxist tradition and shared Marxist desires. However, by the time of *Libidinal Economy*, Lyotard has turned against his old self. He still shares an interest in the intensity of those desires and feelings but no longer accepts the fixed theoretical framework in which they have been constrained. The sections on *Socialisme ou Barbarie*, in *Libidinal Economy*, exhibit this turn against a former self in a graphic and impassioned style: 'so that [our readers] consider our flight into libidinal economy for what it is, the solution to a long pain and the breach out of a difficult impasse'.

In the writing on Marx, Lyotard seeks to make Marx libidinal, not merely in the sense of insisting on the desires and feelings within Marxist theory, but in the sense that those desires and feelings are shown to belong to other parts of the libidinal economy – to the capitalist economic system, for instance. The outcome of Lyotard's somewhat strange and wild reading of Marx is an understanding of political economy as libidinal economy. This involves a subversion of what Lyotard takes to be the main desires of Marxist political economy:

> It would make us happy to be able to retranscribe, into a libidinal dis-
> course, those intensities which haunt Marx's thought and which, in gen-
> eral, are dissimulated in the brass-tacks solemnity of the discourses of
> economy and politics. We will show, therefore, how in Marx's own terms,
> political economy is a libidinal economy. (Lyotard 1993a: 104)

Lyotard's subversion of Marx involves detecting the desires, feelings and affects hidden within Marxist discourse. It also involves releasing the energy of those intensities, from the dispositions which exhaust their energy: 'we must steal [Marx's] affects' (1993a: 103). The central move of Lyotard's strategy here is to split Marx in two, that is, in the terminology of the libidinal economy, to show how two contradictory desires form a duplicitous relation within Marx's discourse. The way this strategy is expressed can appear somewhat extreme when compared to the style of Marxist theoretical discourse, but it makes sense in the light of Lyotard's aim of releasing libidinal intensity. His style contributes to that aim by drawing Marx into a humorous and charged description. The two desires dissimulated within Marx's discourse are represented by two figures: the little girl Marx and the great prosecutor Marx. The little girl is driven by a desire for a 'great love', a true, honest, just and chaste lover, who will devote himself to her alone in a pursuit of happiness. This girl is on the rebound from a terrible, unfaithful and dissolute lover, the Capitalist System; he has betrayed her and spread his body around wherever pleasure took him. The great Marx sets out to right this terrible wrong, to mount a case against the dissolute lover and to find a true love for the little girl. The little girl represents all the just social desires in Marx's discourse: the desire for social cohesion and an end to alienation and exploitation. The great Marx represents the desire for knowledge of the capitalist system and for the deduction of the downfall of that system in favour of a unified and just social system (a new social cohesion, based on the proletariat, the little girl Marx's true lover).

However, behind this desire to supply the girl with a true love there is another more powerful desire, the desire to continue to work on the capitalist system, to continue to capture this ever-changing dissolute flux of intensities in an infinite theory. The great Marx has himself fallen for capitalism, for its power to alter in the face of new intensities. The desires of the little girl and of the great prosecutor, therefore, pull against one another. This is their strength. The little girl's passions are all the stronger because they cannot be satisfied; she can revel in the role of the betrayed lover. The great man's passions are equally delicately poised; he desires what he does not desire, a tantalising and pleasurable postponement of the moment of release:

> the prosecutor charged with obtaining proof of the pornographic igno-
> miny of capital repeats, in his enquiry and even in his preparation and
> pleading, this same 'Don't come yet' – so to speak – which is simply
> another modality of *jouissance*, which is found in the libidinal *dispositif* of
> capital. (1993a: 99)

The libidinal intensity in Marx does not come from the desire for release or for a true love. It comes from a postponement of that release and truth – intensity in Marx is in the preparation for the revolution, not in the revolution itself. Lyotard, in order to encourage the intensity of Marx's discourse, will foster this tension between desires. The point will be not to push Marx towards a resolution, a just overcoming of the capitalist system, but to maintain him within that system.

Lyotard goes through many aspects of Marx's discourse in order to describe Marxist political economy as a libidinal economy. Each time, the point is to dissimulate Lyotard's desire for intensities within Marxist desires. Each time, Lyotard seeks to intensify the tension between the desire for a cohesive and unified society and the fascination with the theoretical study of the many guises and intensities of the capitalist system. It is not possible here to go into all the aspects of the description of political economy as a libidinal economy, so I will concentrate on one of them: the description of the desire for a non-alienated society as a desire that cannot be satisfied. This description takes place in the sections entitled 'There is no subversive region' and 'Every political economy is libidinal' in *Libidinal Economy*. The titles indicate how the libidinal economy does not allow for a special region that would subvert its duplicitous processes into a well-regulated economy, free of the dissimulations, duplicities and tensions of the libidinal band proper. Such a region is the dream of the little girl Marx.

It is also, according to Lyotard, the dream of contemporary philosophers such as Jean Baudrillard in *The Mirror of Production*. According to Lyotard, Baudrillard dreams of an economy free of production for profit and free of value, free of libidinal greed and desire. This economy would be one free of interest and the search for profit; it would resemble a society of 'good savages' or 'good hippies'. For Lyotard, there are no such subversive societies, because the desire at work in their primitive exchanges must be duplicitous, it must involve tensions between, for example, a self-interest and a social concern. For Lyotard, any economy must dissimulate the energy of intensities and intensities can give rise to any desires. Even when we share Marxist goals, we must not forget that intensities are events. To posit an original subversive society free of the range of desires harnessed by the capitalist system is a mistake. In Lyotard's words, economies are always scrambled:

'Scrambled' means that the economy of desire cannot be attributed [to a region], just like ambivalence, not only because it is Eros and the death drive, but because the effects of each instance are inascribable . . . *There is as much libidinal intensity in capitalist exchange as in the alleged 'symbolic' exchange.* (1993a: 109)

Libidinal economy and capital

Does this rejection of systems that seek their independence from capitalism imply that Lyotard's philosophy favours the capitalist economic system? The answer, developed in *Libidinal Economy* and in 'Capitalism energumen' and 'Notes sur le retour et le capital', both in *Des Dispositifs pulsionnels*, has to be positive and negative. The capitalist economic system, like all dispositions in the libidinal economy, involves duplicitous drives. In its case, Lyotard describes a drive to exploit energy wherever and in whatever form it may appear and a negative and contradictory drive to compare all forms of intensity through the medium of a price, of a value. In simple terms, the entrepreneurial side of the capitalist economic system, or Capital, sees the energy of each feeling or desire as an opportunity, as something to be exploited. But the regulative, systematic, side of Capital needs to bring these individual desires and feelings into the system, through the power of comparison of monetary value. Therefore, Capital has a death drive, the drive to bend everything to a common measure, and an Eros, the drive to move into novel zones, to discover new opportunities.

For the libidinal philosopher, Capital is very close to the desire to be good conductors of intensities. But at the same time it is utterly opposed to that desire, through the drive to reduce intensities to comparable units. In accordance with the findings of libidinal economy, these two contradictory aspects are duplicitously entwined in money. Money is both a common measure and a flexible tool that seeks out the greatest return. These aspects cannot be torn apart: the point of the desire to invest in new desires and feelings is monetary profit, the very thing that will then reduce their power. Lyotard describes money as the duplicitous relation between two uses: first, a reproductive use, where its power of comparison is used to provide favourable conditions for the reproduction of products; second, a pillaging use, where its power to invest new regions of the libidinal band, its power to return the highest profits, is used to increase wealth and intensity. For example, a new pharmaceutical product enjoys a period where great profits can be made, until the patent runs out, then profits will diminish. At first, the pharmaceutical company is driven by the desire for profits associated with a novel, highly charged part of the libidinal band. Later, that part is assimilated to all other well-measured parts, through the desire of other companies to reproduce the initial discovery, and its intensity diminishes.

Lyotard's descriptions of monetary economic relations are mostly in terms of sexual practices. He does not allow economic relations to precede all others. Rather, the precedence of the libidinal is asserted, even in economics. The descriptions in terms of sexual practices show the work of the libidinal economics in monetary economics. In the case of the capitalist economic system, a parallel is drawn with classical Chinese erotics. Lyotard is interested in the will to preserve and draw out intensity in the sexual act. The man seeks to reserve his semen by avoiding ejaculation, while drawing on the bodily fluids of the woman – Lyotard claims that the inverse is also possible, that is, the woman can also seek to reserve the man's sexual fluids. Thus the goal of the sexual and economic acts is to excite as much intensity as possible on the other's body, while reserving one's own:

> Not only is emission, that is expenditure, suspended, which is the saving; but the augmentation of forces, for which the penis no longer operates as an escape route for the over-full, but, in the opposite sense, as a drilling channel through which the energetic substances dormant in the folds of the body (of the earth woman) are gathered up . . . (Lyotard 1993a: 209)

Economies are libidinal and so-called natural acts are economic. A libidinal economist, a philosopher whose goal is to act so as to encourage intensities, will act within the capitalist economic system so as to encourage it to seek intensities on all parts of the libidinal band: 'Very little would make all the difference: the conducting of intensities should be able to take place on *all* the pieces of the social "body", without exception' (1993a: 244).

5
Methodology

Methodological problems

There are two main methodological problems implied by Lyotard's descriptions of society. The first concerns the problem of how to handle his description of events so as to allow for a rethinking of political action. The second concerns the problem of how to take account of his description of absolute difference, again with a view to reflecting on the possibility of political action. These obstacles are raised at the very heart of Lyotard's philosophy in its recurring themes (the limits of representation; the event; absolute difference; and the avant-garde). The first, second and the third are the relevant ones here. They are present in Lyotard's descriptions of the libidinal economy where intensities – feelings and desires – are described as events beyond representation and where the incompossibility of figures is described as an absolute difference. They are present in the description of the postmodern condition where phrases and the feeling of the sublime are described as events and where the incommensurability of language games is described as an absolute difference. In both cases, concrete developments on difficult topics bring logical problems into the practical description of an actual state of society. Lyotard's methodology has to find solutions to the logical problems as well as solutions to specific practical problems. I will therefore give both versions of the obstacles. The practical version is perhaps the best for understanding why they cause such problems for Lyotard's final aim of the philosophical political act. The logical version is the best for an understanding of the radical nature of the obstacles, that is, why they are so severe.

The obstacles are as follows (logical formulation (a) first, practical formulation (b) second):

1   (a) If events are beyond representation and understanding, how can they be referred to with certainty?
(b) What is the practical use of things that can neither be satisfactorily referred to nor predicted?
2   (a) How can we know that two things are absolutely different given that such knowledge involves the ability to compare them in a similar way?
(b) What is the practical significance of an absolute difference between two things given that any action on both involves some sort of comparison?

The first problem occurs with the wish to refer with certainty to something that is supposed to be beyond our powers of representation, that is, beyond the capacity of language to capture things. The problem takes the form of a double bind or dilemma. We can either speak of a thing as if we have a clear understanding of it and hence break the statement on the impossibility of representation. Or we can respect that statement, but then we must stay silent and the thing must remain outside the realm of communication.

Lyotard's thought around the theme of the event puts him in such a logical double bind. If, as he says, events are in some way beyond representation, then how can he refer to them with certainty? This becomes a practical problem because his philosophy depends so much on the event. Lyotard makes constant references to events in order to undermine beliefs in the capacity of language and structures to capture all types of experience.

The second problem is similar to the first in so far as it also involves the capacity of language or representation to capture things. In this case, the problem occurs whenever any thinker or writer wishes to affirm that two things are absolutely different. The problem is that this affirmation is made from a single standpoint; it involves a single agent describing the two things in the same medium. This medium is therefore the basis for the deduction of a common ground between the two 'absolutely different' things: they can be captured in a same medium by a single agent. Furthermore, what we know about the medium and the agent will then form the basis for more complex comparisons: 'the two things can be seen by humans and described in the English language', for instance. Again, Lyotard's theme of absolute difference is open to this kind of analysis, that is, any stated difference is at the same time the basis for the deduction of a common ground. The practical repercussions of this logical point are that his many arguments for absolute differences find themselves to be bases for comparisons.

It is important here to note the role played by the demand for certainty and absolute difference in Lyotard's philosophy. Lyotard is always interested, in the first instance, in the search for certainty and in the thwarting of that search. His philosophy opposes a description of the material state of society to the absolutist aim of certainty. Perhaps this interest is driven by his understanding of the demand for certainty in extremely difficult cases. When an activist has to consider injustice and violence on the grand scale, as in Lyotard's Algeria fighting for its independence from France, for example, the measures that may enter into consideration seem to demand certainty. What is more, solutions put forward to dire problems are often presented as based on certainty; perhaps they have to be, given the sacrifices they tend to demand. If we are to deal in matters of life and death, surely we ought to be certain?

Lyotard's answer to this question is in the negative because he believes that there can be no such certainty. However, the result of this drive against certainty is a paradoxical involvement in the search for absolutes. Lyotard's own philosophy has to deal in absolutes in order to confound the search for certainty. He seeks to prove – with as much certainty as possible – that certainty is impossible. The difficult testimony for events beyond representation and the affirmation of absolute difference come from this paradox. Perhaps this also explains why Lyotard's philosophy is so far removed from pragmatic compromise, even though his suspicion of certainty would seem consistent with such a position. He cannot easily turn to pragmatic philosophical political acts, because he is aware of the power of certainty and of the need to eliminate that power. His dedication to the philosophical political act, in the most extreme and difficult of cases, and his opposition to those who offer certainty on those cases, pushes Lyotard into the paradox of having to prove with certainty that there can be no such thing.

Lyotard's difficulties with pragmatism are reflected in Richard Rorty's ambivalent reaction to his philosophy. Rorty identifies with Lyotard's renunciation of grand narratives, the search for absolute certainty and universal truths. Yet he wishes to distance himself from the desire to dismiss them with absolute certainty. In particular, where Lyotard tries to convince us of the incommensurability of language games and dispositions, Rorty's pragmatism seeks a consensus which is not grounded on any grand narrative. Rorty attempts to express this problematic relation through an appeal to a median between the positions of Lyotard and Habermas:

> I can summarize my attempt to split the difference between Lyotard and Habermas by saying that this Deweyan attempt to make concrete concerns with the daily problems of one's community – social engineering – the substitute for traditional religion seems to me to embody Lyotard's postmodernist 'incredulity towards metanarratives' while dispensing with the assumption that the intellectual has a mission to be avant-garde, to escape the rules and practices and institutions which have been transmitted to her in favour of something which make possible 'authentic criticism'. (Rorty 1991: 175)

This selective philosophy makes sense from the point of view of Rorty's pragmatism, but it clashes violently with the logic of Lyotard's philosophy. The incredulity towards metanarratives only makes sense from the point of view of a philosophy of the event, the feeling of the sublime and incommensurable language games. Rorty's desire for social consensus outweighs the philosophical desire for truth. This allows him to dismiss Lyotard's work on the sublime as an irrelevance, while he adopts the work on metanarratives: 'But this quest [for the sublime] is wildly irrelevant to the attempt at communicative consensus which is the vital force which drives [bourgeois] culture' (Rorty 1991: 176). This description of the event of an avant-garde work of art in an attempt at communicative consensus is wildly at odds with Lyotard's definition of the sublime. In turn, this misunderstanding focuses attention on the distance that separates Lyotard's work on metanarratives and Rorty's pragmatism. Where Lyotard struggles with the obstacles presented by the paradoxes of the event and absolute difference, Rorty is happy to ignore philosophical problems in the name of consensus. At least from the point of view of the interpretation of Lyotard's philosophy, the limits of this pragmatism are clear: it sacrifices the recognition of difference for superficial agreement.

The two obstacles outlined above are a useful tool in any analysis of Lyotard's philosophy because they go deep into the detail of his methodology. For example, the logical and practical versions of the first obstacle are replicated in Lyotard's study of the event as feeling or phrase. In these cases, the problem becomes: 'How can Lyotard describe events, which cannot be represented with certainty, as feelings or phrases and then make certain statements about feelings and phrases?' This process of replication is particularly difficult to escape. Whenever the philosopher tries to define a term that escapes the first obstacles, it will be replicated in a new version applicable to the new case.

This process can be seen at its most powerful where attempts are made to avoid the problem through the definition of terms that can only be represented in part. Such attempts seek a partial grasp on that which cannot be represented or understood in full; this part is then grasped 'by proxy' through a part which can be represented. An example of this would be the reference to signs, as in the statement 'This thing is a sign of something beyond representation.' The process of replication can be seen through a new set of questions on the dividing line, the limit between the representable and non-representable parts. It is hard for Lyotard to escape questions such as 'How does the sign represent that which cannot be represented?' and 'If the sign is related to something beyond representation and understanding, then how can we know that our understanding or representation of the sign is complete?' The attempt to capture that which is beyond representation through that which is not falls prey to a process of reversal, that is, what is supposed to be within the bounds of representation is caught up with that which is beyond representation. The limit between the two can never be clear-cut or certain because one side of the limit is beyond the powers of understanding and representation.

So, for Lyotard, it will never be satisfactory to merely answer that phrases and feelings are known in part, or can be described in part. This answer will always raise a further set of obstacles around the limit between the two parts. For instance, where Lyotard calls phrases events, the following questions arise: 'If phrases are events, then on what grounds can there be any certain claims to understand or represent what they are?' and 'If events are phrases, then does our certain understanding and representation of phrases not provide us with a certain understanding of events?' The questions drive at a new version of the initial obstacle, where the problem has been transferred to questions about phrases, instead of questions about events. This shift is all the more serious given the precision with which phrases can be defined, as 'a mode of expression' or 'a small group of words', for example. These definitions form the basis for an ever-improving representation and understanding of phrases; how then can Lyotard claim that they are beyond representation or that they cannot be fully understood? It would appear, then, that the two main obstacles to his philosophy, based on developments of the themes of the event and absolute difference, are replicated within many of his attempts to avoid them.

It would be a mistake, though, to base criticisms of Lyotard's philosophy only on versions of the two objections set out above. His philosophy does not only displace the main problems on to new but similar grounds, thereby leaving itself open to replications of the problem. Rather, Lyotard's strategy is to present the 'problem' as something unavoidable, as a factor inextricably linked to the matter at hand for philosophy, to an actual state of society. An illustration of the thinking behind this strategy can be seen in the following quote, where Lyotard notes that some forms of wrong done to people lead to a double bind or dilemma. In these cases the wrong is to be unable to speak of the wrong:

> Either you are a victim of the wrong, or you are not. If you are not, you are deceived (or lying) in testifying that you are. If you are, since you can bear witness to this wrong, it is not a wrong, and you are deceived (or lying) in testifying that you are a victim of the wrong. . . . The ancients called this argument a dilemma. It contains the mechanism of the *double bind*. (Lyotard 1988a: 5)

It is Lyotard's view that there are cases which lead to this unjust position; in effect, his own understanding of the event puts him in such a position. A further development of this view is that the obstacles must be taken into account instead of eliminated. The problems can only be considered as avoidable if certain theories of representation, understanding, language and general structures are held to be true. Lyotard's philosophy is an attempt to show that they are not. It is also an attempt to put forward alternative philosophies of language, representation and structural organization. His strategic methodology is therefore not only a response to the two main objections concerning events and absolute difference; it is also a development of philosophies of language, representation and structure. This development takes place in the knowledge that there can be no such thing as certainty in matters that concern the actual states of society.

The question is 'How does Lyotard know this?' Answers to this question come from the philosophy of language that underpins Lyotard's description of the postmodern condition and the philosophy of structural disorganization that underpins his description of the libidinal economy. These philosophies put forward responses to the two main objections given above, not only as displacements of the problems raised in the objections, but also as challenges to the very basis on which they are judged to be problems. Of course, because it challenges an established view of language and structure, Lyotard's work can only be called 'philosophy of language' or 'philosophy of structure' with the proviso that language and structure be understood in the new sense dictated by his work.

Lyotard's philosophy of language

Lyotard's philosophy of language is developed in conjunction with his description of the postmodern condition. The point of the philosophy of language, set out in Lyotard's *The Differend*, will be to show how practical difficulties in the description can be avoided and to show how corresponding logical problems do not apply to his philosophy. These solutions can be seen as a defence of Lyotard's description of the postmodern condition. They show how Lyotard's description is consistent and how his political acts are devised on a firm basis. The specific problems addressed in the philosophy of language are:

1 How to justify the assertion that all phrases are events?
2 How to explain the incommensurability of language games or genres?

In effect, these problems challenge Lyotard to express his beliefs on events and absolute difference in a linguistic structure. He will have to show that language, the way we communicate, allows for the occurrence of events and the existence of absolute differences between things. This is no trivial challenge: language is often seen as a medium and mediator between people; it is also seen as a way of referring to things in the world. These properties would seem to go counter to what he has to show. How does a language as medium for communication, as a way of breaking down barriers, allow for absolute differences? We use language in debates and dialogues, and these allow us to understand one another. If there is such a thing as an absolute difference, then surely it must be extra linguistic? We also use language to refer to things, for example when we use a proper name. Does this use not provide us with a way of fixing our understanding of phrases by referring them to the world? Can we not devise ways of representing phrases in terms of what they mean or in terms of our understanding of them through a reference to what they refer to?

The philosophy of language in *The Differend* responds to these problems and questions in five steps:

1   a rejection of the thesis that phrases can be fixed through a reference to an outside reality;
2   a definition of phrases as events, as things which cannot be fully understood or represented;
3   the deduction of the law of concatenation: 'To link on from phrases is necessary but how to link is not';
4   a demonstration of how phrases, defined as events, can give rise to genres or language games;
5   a demonstration of how language games must be incommensurable.

For Lyotard, everything can be understood as a phrase, but phrases cannot be fully understood. This is because each phrase is an event. We cannot know how to link other phrases on to it, and yet such links constitute an understanding and a representation of the initial sentence. So there is no right concatenation. Neither is there a way of tending towards a right concatenation; the search for relatively correct trends in the linking of phrases is also defeated by the status of phrases as events. For example, it is not possible to move towards a full understanding of phrases – and hence, to a knowledge of the right concatenations – by directing our attention to the things a phrase is supposed to refer to. It is wrong to think that communication depends on the reference to an outside world. Rather, phrases refer to each other according to the rules governing their concatenation. Any act following the phrase event is a link and these links can be seen as following rules or norms. These rules or norms define language games or genres. However, because there is no such thing as the right concatenation, genres are incommensurable with respect to the certain or just way of following on from an event. There is therefore no way of determining which set of rules, which genre, is the right one to govern a concatenation of phrases. It is possible for there to be successful communication, because there are genres whose rules can allow us to determine relative success, but this does not mean that it is possible for there to be more or less right concatenations.

Phrases, genres and the differend

Thus, according to Lyotard, there is no such thing as the right link in a chain of communications; each phrase in a debate, dialogue, monologue or succession of events is open to an infinite number of equally right responses. A phrase occurs and other phrases are linked on to it according to rules supplied by different genres: 'A phrase "happens". How can it be linked onto? By its rule, a genre of discourse supplies a set of possible phrases, each arising from some other phrase regimen.' However, no genre provides the absolutely correct or right way of linking on from the initial phrase. This means genres can supply a conflicting set of concatenations or links on from the initial phrase – these conflicts are differends: 'Another genre of discourse supplies another set of other possible phrases. There is a differend between these two sets (or between the genres that call them forth) because they are heterogeneous' (Lyotard 1988a: xii). But where is the practical stake in all this?

It is in the conflicts between language games. Lyotard calls them differends: irresolvable conflicts that arise between language games when they have to determine the right way to follow on from any given phrase or event. The aim of his politics will be to testify to the existence of differends against those theories and actions that deny them. His politics is in opposition to the philosophies, systems and practices that affirm right ways of pursuing a dialogue, right ways of resolving conflicts through debates. This affirmation involves a right concatenation or a trend towards right concatenations. It champions a set of rules, a language game or genre, allowing us to tend towards what is right in any circumstance. Lyotard, on the contrary, champions the differend, the possibility of many different and equally right concatenations entering into conflict over a same initial phrase event. This is how a strategic methodology leads to a strategic teleology, a philosophical politics:

> 184. Let's recapitulate (Nos 180, 181): a phrase comes along. What will be its fate, to what end will it be subordinated, within what genre of discourse will it take its place? No phrase is the first. This does not only mean that others precede it, but also that the modes of linking implied in the previous phrases – possible modes of linking therefore – are ready to take the phrases into account and to inscribe in the pursuit of certain stakes, to actualize themselves by means of it. In this sense, a phrase that comes along is put into play within a conflict between genres of discourse. This conflict is a differend, since the success (or the validation) proper to one genre is not the one proper to others. (1988a: 136)

The political import of the differend will be as a conflict or legal dispute that cannot be resolved through an appeal to a particular language game and set of rules. All a particular language game can achieve is a covering up of the initial conflict or differend. This can be done by arbitrarily eliminating one of the participants, or by coming to a resolution of the conflict that is unfair to one or both of them. Lyotard distinguishes a case of just litigation, where there is no conflict between genres, and a differend, where there is a conflict between at least two parties. In the case of a litigation there can be a just resolution, whereas in the case of a differend there is a 'lack of a rule of judgement applicable to both arguments. One side's legitimacy does not imply the other's lack of legitimacy' (1988a: xi). But in a judgement a single rule must be applied, this means that the judge must take sides with one of the parties or be unjust to both. A resolution that satisfies both parties is impossible.

The problem of reference

Lyotard's belief in the differend must involve a scepticism towards resolutions of conflict through an appeal to evidence, to 'what really happened'. This shows the importance of his rejection of reality, of the reference to the outside world, as a way of fixing our understanding of phrases. The first point in the philosophy of language is a move to distance phrases from the things they refer to. This is done in an analysis of the vehicles for reference: proper names. Lyotard argues that proper names in a phrase do not refer to an outside reality that can be inspected through 'a process of verification', but rather, that reality is constituted by the conjunction of the various senses that the phrase can have and the thing to which the name refers. So the name does not have a sense of its own that can be fixed by referring to a real thing in the world. Instead, there is a series of different versions of reality, brought forth when a name brings a thing that is referred to together with a network of senses, that is, the different senses of the phrase that includes the name.

We cannot understand the sense of the proper name 'Fidel Castro' by inspecting the Fidel Castro we encounter in the world. The act of ostension, to show Fidel Castro, is never sufficient for the constitution of reality. For Lyotard, the name 'Fidel Castro' can have no sense on its own; sense is a property of phrases or chains of phrases. So reality comes from the conjunction of phrases and rigid designators, names rigidly designating a particular thing:

> Reality cannot be deduced from sense alone, no more than it can from
> ostension alone. It does not suffice to conclude that the two are required
> together. It must be shown how the ostensive *This is it*, and the descrip-
> tive, *It is the city which is the capital of the Empire*, are articulated into: *This is
> the city which is the capital of the Empire*. The name holds the position of
> linchpin. Rome is substitutes for the deictic (*This is Rome*) and takes the
> place of the referent in the descriptive (*Rome is the city which is the capital of
> the Empire*). . . . The name fills the function of linchpin because it is an
> empty and constant designator. (1988a: 44)

Only phrases or chains of phrases can have sense. Reality is constituted when a proper name brings those senses in contact with a
referent, the thing that is referred to. For Lyotard, the proper name is
empty, by itself it has no sense; he calls it a rigid designator – it
designates or refers to specific things. Reality has now become a
function of phrases as well as of things in the world: it comes about
when empty rigid designators link a referent to a sense. It is no longer
possible to claim that an appeal to reality, to what really happened or
what was really the case, can necessarily help to resolve conflicts. This
is because reality itself can be the object of such a conflict.

Names are linchpins through which many different phrases, many
different senses, can be associated with a given thing. The name
itself provides no clue as to which senses can be truly or correctly
associated with the thing it designates. This is because the name is
an empty rigid designator, offering no sense of its own, no information on the thing. This sense or information can only come from
phrases. The result of this is that reality has now become a function
of phrases, of senses. For Lyotard, this means that reality allows for
the competition of different senses over particular things, a competition that cannot be resolved through an appeal to reality. He calls
this conflict that cannot be resolved a differend:

> 92. Reality entails the differend. *That's Stalin, here he is.* We acknowledge
> it. But as for what Stalin means? Phrases come to be attached to this name,
> which not only describe different senses for it (this can still be debated in
> dialogue), and not only place the name on different instances, but which
> also obey different regimens and/or genres. This heterogeneity, for lack
> of a common idiom, makes consensus impossible. The assignment of a
> definition to Stalin necessarily does wrong to the nondefinitional phrases
> relating to Stalin, which this definition, for a while at least, disregards or
> betrays. In and around names vengeance is on the prowl. (1988a: 56)

Having explained Lyotard's use of names as rigid designators, it
is worth pointing out that his study of the linguistic function of

names does not go into great depth. He has taken much of his terminology from other philosophers of language, but he has not made the same careful analytic distinctions, or gone through the same empirical studies as they have (the term 'rigid designator', for example, owes much to Saul Kripke's *Naming and Necessity*). This is a particular weakness of Lyotard's work on the philosophy of language; he is apt to sketch his point with little regard to the detailed study of what it entails. He alludes to the great debates and texts of the philosophy of language, to Russell and Frege on reference, for example, but he does not go into the substance of these difficult debates with any systematicity.

Two conclusions can be drawn from this lack. First, Lyotard's philosophy of language does not really stand up by itself; its importance is as a sketchy theoretical framework for the wider conclusions drawn in his philosophy of events and of their impact on any political act. Second, Lyotard's philosophy has an Achilles heel where he draws on philosophy of language to support his wider philosophy. It is open to attacks from other deeper and more systematic studies. These point are made most forcefully and on the basis of a deep knowledge of Wittgenstein's work in Jacques Bouveresse, *Rationalité et cynisme* (1984: 107-84).

Independent of any doubts about the thoroughness of Lyotard's study of names and their relation to reality, two questions arise from his sketch of their role as linchpins between sense and referents. The first question is technical: it asks for an explanation of how phrases allow for sense to be associated with a referent through a proper name. In effect, it asks 'How do phrases work?' The second question is philosophical and critical: it is a question about the feasibility of Lyotard's wider project. The question is: 'How does Lyotard's response to the first question allow him to maintain that it is not possible to determine the right phrase to follow any specific phrase, given that it is possible to determine the sense the initial phrase associates with a referent?'

The complexity of this latter question can be bypassed if it is looked at in practical terms. Imagine that archaeologists claim that no one will ever be able to work out the right interpretation of a mysterious inscription on an ancient artefact. This will be a fairly acceptable claim so long as they give a good reason for their affirmation, for example that there is no other evidence from the time of the artefact and hence no other possible reference point. However, imagine that they also maintain that the inscription had a crucial and quite specific role to play in religious ceremonies. Then we will begin to lose confidence in the first claim, because we will be in a position to begin to determine the meaning of the inscription, through a reference to its function in the ceremonies for example.

Lyotard is in the same position as the archaeologists. So long as he does not give us a clue as to the sense of phrases, his claim as to the impossibility of determining the right concatenations seems to stand up. But once he begins to flesh out his theory of phrases, his original claim is in danger of collapse, because he will have provided a frame of reference for the determination of right concatenations, or at least, more or less right ones. It is also worth noting that the archaeologist example can be analysed in terms of the main obstacles to Lyotard's project, that is, if the archaeologists can discount the possibility of any further discoveries concerning their artefact, then they must know many things about the artefact. Will it not be possible, therefore, to put that knowledge to work in deciphering it?

Presentation and situation

Lyotard's solution to these questions involves an important distinction drawn between two ways in which phrases work: the distinction between a *presentation* and a *situation*. He argues that any phrase presents at least one universe but that the relation between the various elements of the universe only becomes fixed once it is situated. A universe brings together a sense, a referent (a thing that is referred to, whether a real thing or an imaginary one), an addressor (the thing from which the sentence is deemed to come) and an addressee (the thing to which the sentence is deemed to be going):

> 111. A phrase presents at least one universe. No matter which regimen it obeys, it entails a There is [*Il y a*]. There is what is signified, what it is signified about, to whom and by whom it is signified: a universe. *At least* one universe, because the sense, the referent, the addressor, or the addressee can be equivocal. (Lyotard 1988a: 70)

This is Lyotard's explanation for the association of a sense and a referent in a phrase. The universe presented by the phrase allows for the association of the sense and the referent in a communication going from an addresser to an addressee. Phrases may present more than one universe because the four elements of the presentation, Lyotard calls them instances, can be equivocal, uncertain or open. For example, a phrase may present a universe in such a way as to leave the addressee unknown (this would be true of books as opposed to personal letters). However, presentation entailed by a phrase does not allow for the meaning of the phrase to be fixed. It leaves no clues as to how to follow the phrase with another. Although the phrase presents a universe made up of the four instances, this presentation is entirely open as to how the instances fit together. Until we know the relation, we will not be in a position to know the right way to follow the sentence. This fit, Lyotard argues, only takes place in a situation, that is, when the initial phrase is included in a concatenation:

> 115. A presentation is that there is at least one universe. A situation is that at the heart of a universe presented by a phrase, relations indicated by the form of the phrases that link onto it (through the phrases regimen, which calls forth certain linkings) place the instances in relation to each other. (1988a: 71)

Lyotard has constructed a way out of the problem given above. He explains that it is possible for phrases to bear meaning because they present a universe. Yet it is not possible to know the right way of following the phrase until the instances of the universe are related to one another in a fixed manner. This relation is dependent on the situation of those instances, but a situation can only take place when the initial sentence is included in a concatenation, that is, when another sentence follows it.

For example, the phrase 'One day we will understand the importance of Fidel Castro' presents at least the one universe. This universe includes you the addressee, me the addressor, Fidel Castro the referent and the sense *One day we will understand the importance of Fidel Castro*. But how these instances are related depends on the phrases I am writing now. Do you know yet whether the example is about the specifics of Lyotard's philosophy of language, about the relation between his philosophy of language and his work on philosophical political action, or whether it marks a turning point in the book towards a denial of theoretical time-wasting and an affirmation of direct action? The initial phrase failed to relate the instances of its presentation; they only became related when further phrases followed on and situated those instances. Now you know the status of the initial phrase, but do you know the status of this phrase? This is Lyotard's point: although 'One day we will know the importance of Fidel Castro' can present instances of at least one universe, those instances will only ever be related to one another when a further phrase intervenes: 'In order to grasp the presentation entailed by a phrase, another phrase is needed, in which this presentation is presented. The "present" presentation is not able to be phrased now; it is only able to be phrased as a situation' (1988a: 74).

The distinction drawn between presentation and situation allows Lyotard to define phrases as events. The phrase occurs and brings forth a presentation, but the presentation can only be grasped when it is situated by a further sentence. This later situation can never grasp the full potential of the initial presentation. It narrows the presentation down to a more specific situation and eliminates many of the possibilities brought forth in the presentation of the initial phrase. This is why phrases are events in Lyotard's sense: they cannot be fully understood or represented because any understanding or representation of the phrase is a situation of its initial presentation. The situation reduces or limits the potential of the initial presentation. For example, take the phrase 'Marry me!' This phrase brings forth many different universes, many different instances or possible addressors, addressees, senses and referents. Each of the possible answers to the phrase limits those instances. The answers 'You must be joking!', 'You're not supposed to propose until line 15 of the script', 'Quoi?' enforce different instances and different arrangements of instances on the original phrase (the sense, for example, varies to some degree from tragic through fake to nonsense).

In *The Differend*, Lyotard deduces the distinction of presentation and situation from difficult technical readings of Kant and Aristotle. He uses Kant's analysis of how objects are given to subjects in intuition to show how, prior to an object being given in intuition, there must be some kind of presentation of it, some kind of pre-intuition. This presentation will not necessarily obey the categories which apply to all objects of intuition. Lyotard uses Aristotle's study of time to show how the present is a moment that is always lost once it is represented as a moment in time, that is, as the moment thought of in relation to the past and the future. The point of his work, here, is to show how any theory of presentation, whether it is Kant's analysis of objects given in intuition or Aristotle's study of the present, is itself a mere situation of presentation. A presentation cannot be wholly understood or represented.

According to Lyotard, in Kant:

The idea of a given (of an immediately given) is a way of receiving and censuring the idea of a presentation. A presentation does not present a universe to someone; it is the event of its (inapprehensible) presence. A given is given to a subject, who receives it and deals with it. To deal with it is to situate it, to place it in a phrase universe. (1988a: 61)

Similarly, Aristotle according to Lyotard,

distinguishes time which, in universes presented by phrases, situates the instances constituting these universes in relation to each other (the before/after, the now), from the presentation-event (or occurrence) which as such is absolute (now). As soon as one phrases the latter, it is placed among the relations of phrase universes. (1988a: 74)

We cannot capture the present moment – the 'now'– in time. Once we see the present as related to the past and to the future, something important has been lost. Neither can we capture a presentation through an analysis of it as a presented object given to us in intuition. Something happens. But when we try to understand that thing in relation to the framework we depend on to fix objects, a grid of colours and possible shapes for example, something of the initial presentation has been lost. According to Lyotard, these same conclusions apply to phrases. A phrase brings forth a presentation, this presentation is lost once it becomes a situation, that is, when a phrase follows on from the initial one and places it in a specific concatenation.

Once again, it is important to stress the mercenary aspects of Lyotard's use of Kant and Aristotle. Lyotard appeals to the works of other philosophers in order to make points which are entirely his own. This means that although his reading of other philosophers may be productive and interesting in the way it brings their work into his perspective, the interpretation is often partial and tendentious. Lyotard's relation to the philosophical tradition is one of productive exploitation not one of objective assessment or careful restoration. However, this is not to question the value and originality of his detailed works on figures from the history of philosophy. In particular, his studies of Marx, Freud and Kant stand as illuminating and important additions to the scholarship in these fields. See, for example, Lyotard's excellent study of Kant's critical philosophy in *L'Enthousiasme* (1986) and his reworking of Freud and Marx in *Dérive à partir de Marx et Freud* (1973), partly translated as *Driftworks*.

There are many possible situations of a single presentation. A presentation is brought forth by a phrase; this presentation involves at least one universe comprising the instances of addressor, addressee, sense and referent. The exact relation between these instances is only set once a further phrase follows the initial one. But this initial phrase has the status of an event: it is beyond representation and cannot be wholly understood. This means that we cannot determine exactly the right phrase to follow any given phrase, we cannot determine the right situation of the initial presentation. This fact allows Lyotard to deduce his law of concatenation, the law governing the linking of phrases: 'To link is necessary, but how to link is not.' The first part of the deduction depends on the strange assertion that anything that follows a phrase is a further phrase and hence involves a situation of the initial one. Thus, for Lyotard, to pass over a phrase in silence is to link another phrase to it: 'For *And a phrase* to be necessary signifies that the absence of a phrase (a silence, etc.) or the absence of a linkage (the beginning, the end, disorder, nothingness, etc.) are also phrases' (Lyotard 1988a: 68).

The odd assertion that apparently extralinguistic things can be phrases is made possible by Lyotard's use of the terms presentation and situation. It is possible for apparently extralinguistic things such as silence to be phrases because they do bring forth a presentation. The silence of someone with the power to pardon prior to an execution brings forth at least one universe: the monarch, say, the executioner, the convict and the order to execute. It also situates a prior phrase, such as 'Shall I put him to death?' The silent telephone sets off and completes chains of events as well as any linguistic phrase.

It is therefore impossible to escape having to follow a phrase of which we are possible addressees. Worse, although we have to act – because even our inaction is an action – we cannot know the right way to act. Any phrase that we may use will situate the initial presentation on shaky grounds. This is because we cannot fully understand or represent the initial phrase, the trigger for our action: 'For there to be no phrase is impossible, for there to be *And a Phrase* is necessary. It is necessary to make linkage. . . . To link is necessary, but how to link is not' (1988a: 66). This is the law of concatenation; it brings uncertainty into Lyotard's political philosophy. At one stroke, action has become something we cannot avoid and something we cannot determine for certain. There are many different ways in which we can follow on from the presentation brought forth by a particular phrase, and none of these ways is absolutely right. Philosophy and philosophical politics have thereby lost the possibility of an appeal to understanding, be that the understanding of phrases, of the world, of consciousness, as a basis for certain political action. Instead, what we have are many different bases with no common measure to judge them by. These differences will give rise to differends, conflicts that cannot be resolved in an absolutely just manner.

They are also the differences at the basis of Lyotard's analysis of the postmodern condition: the conflict of incommensurable language games. Language games have no common measure with respect to the right way of following a given event. With the deduction of the law of concatenation, Lyotard has answered one of the questions arising out of his description of the postmodern condition, 'How can there be absolute difference?' There can be absolute difference because different ways of linking on from a given event cannot be measured or judged by referring to that event: 'A phrase, which links and which is to be linked, is always a *pagus*, a border zone where genres of discourse enter into a conflict over the mode of linking' (1988a: 151).

Incommensurability and heterogeneity

In *The Differend* the somewhat vague concept of incommensurable language games from *The Postmodern Condition* is replaced by the concepts of incommensurable or heterogeneous (Lyotard has an unfortunate tendency to use both terms in similar circumstances) phrase regimens and genres. Phrase regimens are the different syntactic types phrases can belong to. A phrase can be descriptive, cognitive, prescriptive, evaluative, interrogative and so on (the phrase then involves a description, imparts knowledge, involves an order, an evaluation, a question). Each regimen defines a phrase as demanding a certain type of link. For example, a prescriptive phrase such as 'Charge!' is determined by an act obeying the prescription, in this case the act of leaving the trenches and entering no man's land. These links help us to know how to follow on from phrases, but there is no necessity in those links, it is perfectly possible for an apparently wrong link to be appropriate in given circumstances, in the example this could be to faint or to argue. The regimen of the initial phrase will then be different (in the case of fainting, it has become a descriptive phrase: one faints because the initial phrase has described the carnage to follow by reminding us of similar bloody cases).

According to Lyotard, phrase regimens are heterogeneous because phrases from different regimens have presented the instances in a universe in radically different ways: 'For every phrase regimen, there corresponds a mode of presenting a universe . . . The universe

presented by a cognitive and the universe presented by an ex-
clamative are heterogeneous' (1988a: 128). Each regimen involves
a different situation of an initial presentation (this is why he uses
the expression presented instead of presentation in the quote
above). The different situations involve different relations between
the instances of the universe brought forth by the initial phrase.
Those situations are then radically different although they are situations of a same presentation. Again, this is because of the law of
concatenation, there is no way of determining a relation between the
many different regimens to which a phrase can belong. The possibilities brought forth by the phrase 'Charge!' are developed and
curtailed in radically different ways by different regimens and there
is no way of determining which is the right way; that is, there is no
way of comparing the different regimens as situations of the initial
presentation. The situations of obedience (going over the top) and of
pathological reaction (fainting) are radically different. There is no
right way of relating them to one another as they describe different
situations and different universes:

> These universes are constituted by the way the instances (not only the
> sense, but also the referent, the addressor and the addressee) are situated
> as well as by their interrelations. The addressor of an exclamative is not
> situated with regard to the sense in the same way as the addressor of a
> descriptive. The addressee of a command is not situated with regard to
> the addressor and to the referent in the same way as the addressee of an
> invitation or of a bit of information is. (1988a: 49)

It is worth noting here how this point is harder to understand
than it should be because of Lyotard's rather awkward use of 'presentation' (*presentation*) and 'presented' (*présentée*) or 'situated' (*située*).
A presentation is brought forth by a phrase – it is only presented
when another phrase comes to follow the initial one. Thus 'presented' indicated a situation rather than a presentation – it is unfortunate that Lyotard did not avoid possible confusion by using
'situated' instead of 'presented' consistently. Still, independently of
these problems, Lyotard shows through the concept of a phrase
regimen how it is possible for absolute differences to occur in chains
of phrases. They occur with respect to a given event or presentation
because different regimens situate the initial presentation in radically different ways. There is no way of comparing one regimen
with another. Although they can be traced back to an initial presentation, they involve heterogeneous situations of the presentation.
    However, although phrase regimens cannot be compared as situ-

ations of an initial presentation, this does not mean that they cannot be compared on any terms. It would be possible to compare two phrases in terms of beauty or truthfulness, for example. However, this form of comparison can only take place in what Lyotard calls a genre of discourse, that is, a set of rules defining particular ways of linking phrases. The genre defines pertinent links, acceptable ways of following one phrase with another. For example, there could be an aesthetic genre, where links were judged as pertinent if they contributed to the general aim of coming to a judgement on what is beautiful. Or there could be a scientific genre, where links were judged as pertinent if they contributed to the general aim of increasing our scientific knowledge of the world. Both cases would involve rules for determining pertinent concatenations. The scientific rule could be that every thesis should be followed by a proof, whereas the aesthetic rule could be that every judgement should be followed by an appeal to taste.

Here we see how Lyotard's definition of genres in *The Differend* rejoins his definition of language games in *The Postmodern Condition*. Both terms relate to the different rule-driven types of discourse referred to in different practical situations. In no way, though, would these rules determine the right links between phrases or the right language game to use in a given practical case. There are many pertinent concatenations and there is no way of judging whether one is right and another is wrong. A link judged as pertinent or valid from within one genre cannot be judged as impertinent or non-valid from within another: 'To link is necessary, but a particular linkage is not. This linkage can be declared pertinent, though, and the phrase that does the stating is a rule for linking' (1988a: 81). The key to the difference between pertinent and right is the law of concatenation. In absolute terms, there is no necessarily right concatenation, there are only pertinent concatenations relative to the rules of different genres. For Lyotard, these absolute terms are always in relation to an initial event or phrase. It is with respect to them that genres are incommensurable. Thus genres of discourse can bring phrases from heterogeneous regimens together in a concatenation. But, again, with respect to the initial heterogeneity of regimens, genres are incommensurable. There is no way of comparing them as ways of linking on from initial events.

Genres of discourse do not only allow us to determine the pertinence of a concatenation, they also introduce the notion of a stake. A simple understanding of these stakes could be that they are what is to be achieved through a particular concatenation. The stakes are the ultimate goal implied by a particular genre:

> 148. The stakes bound up with a genre of discourse determine the linking between phrases. They determine them, however, only as an end may determine the means: by eliminating those that are not opportune. One will not link onto *To arms!* with *You have just formulated a prescription,* if the stakes are to make someone act with urgency. One will do it if the stakes are to make someone laugh. But there are many other means to achieve an end. (Lyotard 1988a: 84)

The introduction of the stakes implied by genres of discourse allows Lyotard to introduce his concept of the differend to his philosophy of language. Different genres will involve different stakes and this will bring them into conflict over how to follow on from an initial phrase. When one genre determines the pertinent link on from a phrase, it has imposed its stake over the stakes of other genres: 'a phrase that comes along is put into play within a conflict between genres of discourse. This conflict is a differend, since the success (or the validation) proper to one genre is not the one proper to others' (1988a: 136) The imposition of one genre over others can never be justified in terms of the correct concatenation because, as I have indicated above, no such concatenation exists: 'The multiplicity of stakes, on a par with the multiplicity of genres, turns every linkage into a kind of "victory" of one of them over the others. These others remain neglected, forgotten, or repressed possibilities' (Lyotard 1988a: 136). The aim of Lyotard's philosophy will be to take account of the conflict of genres in the light of the need to follow an event according to the rules and stake of one genre to the detriment of those of other genres. This conflict is what Lyotard will call the political and it is here that his philosophy will be active: 'Everything is political if politics is the possibility of the differend on the occasion of the slightest linkage' (1988a: 139). The form this action takes will be studied in detail in the next chapter.

The sublime and the differend

At this point, though, it is worth returning to the two problems outlined at the outset of this chapter. First, can Lyotard really show that genres are incommensurable? That is, are they really absolutely different in terms of their rules or stakes? Lyotard states that there are no rules and no stakes which can reconcile the differences between different genres: 'The only necessity is to link onto [the phrase], nothing more. Inside a genre of discourse, the linkings obey rules that determine the stakes and the ends. But between one genre and another, no such rules are known, nor a generalised end' (1988a: 30). This statement is very close to his attack on metanarratives outlined in chapter 2 above. The thing is, it is extremely difficult to prove that no such common stakes or rules can be devised. Apparent differences can often be resolved through an appeal to more profound rules and stakes; when two warring factions in a single nation discover their common cause against an international aggressor, for example. Lyotard's answer here depends entirely on the incommensurability of language games.

Yet, once again, he does not use this term in the same way as the tradition – where philosophers of science such as Kuhn and Feyerabend discuss the incommensurability of scientific theories. Rather, for Lyotard, incommensurability is deduced from the law of concatenation, that is, it is must be thought of in terms of the links between phrases. 'No matter what its regimen, every phrase is in principle what is at stake in a differend between genres of discourse. This differend proceeds from the question, which accompanies any phrase, of how to link onto it' (1988a: 137–8). For Lyotard, genres are incommensurable because they impose concatenations that can never be correct. Genres are to be judged in terms of pertinence or in terms of the stakes they give to a given concatenation. This raises the question, though, of why Lyotard is interested in stakes and rules at all. It would appear that in terms of the linking of phrases all rules and stakes are equally incorrect. If that is so, what does this imply for his own discussion of genres and regimen, presentation and situation? His treatment of various situations and genres from the point of view of the right or correct concatenation is surely an irrelevance given that on these terms all situations and genres are equal?

We are back to the first obstacle: how can Lyotard speak with certainty about those things of which he cannot be certain? Could there not be a clue in the nature of the presentation brought forth by a phrase as to the correct phrase to link on with? How does Lyotard know there is not? It seems that he should ignore the problem of the paradoxical presentation brought forth by a phrase and divert his attention to the relative questions of pertinence and stakes. The problem is, though, how can he know that these problems are relative without his work on presentation? Without the work on presentation there is always the possibility of there being a right genre for any given case. This goes counter to the main themes of Lyotard's work, the event and the limits of representation.

To counter this line of questioning, Lyotard introduces his theory of the sublime. The train of the argument goes as follows:

1   Lyotard's deduction of the incommensurability of genres and of the heterogeneity of regimen depends on the distinction drawn between a presentation and a situation;
2   the distinction comes up against the logical obstacle given at the beginning of this chapter, that is, if there is such a thing as a presentation brought forth by a phrase, we cannot represent it because such a representation would be a situation and not a presentation;
3   this means that Lyotard's philosophy of language loses its main terms, the law of concatenation, the heterogeneity of regimen and the incommensurability of genres;
4   to counter the double bind involved in his concept of presentation, Lyotard puts it in terms of the feeling of the sublime, that is, he argues for a feeling indicating presentation.

The introduction of the feeling of the sublime to *The Differend* marks a turning point in Lyotard's study of the postmodern condition and its relation to the determination of a philosophical political act. As shown by the steps above, the feeling is brought into the philosophy at a point of great stress, where Lyotard has developed his philosophy of language and yet still found it lacking on the key issue of how to represent the unrepresentable: the event. In *The Differend*, this tension shows up where Lyotard enters into an imaginary confrontation with the philosopher Jacques Derrida around the concept of presentation. I will go into some of the background to this conflict, real and imagined, in chapter 8. What is important here is to note Lyotard's reaction to Derrida's formulation of the double bind caused by the distinction drawn between presentation and situation: 'This "reading" is still metaphysical, still subordinate to the hegemony of thought, Derrida would say. Yes, indeed, if it is true that, as a question, time already belongs to metaphysics' (Lyotard 1988a: 74).

By referring to the 'hegemony of thought' in Lyotard's reading of Aristotle on time, Derrida (as played by Lyotard) is drawing attention to the problem that in this reading the moment of the present independent of past and future, the presentation, is still a situation. Lyotard still has to represent and give an understanding of presentation. How can this representation be correct if presentation is beyond representation and understanding? Here is Lyotard's answer:

> The occurrence, the phrase, as a *what* that happens, does not at all stem from the question of time, but from that of Being/non-Being. This question is called forth by a feeling: it is possible for nothing to happen. Silence not as a phrase in abeyance, but as a non-phrase, a non *what*. This feeling is anxiety or surprise: there is something rather than nothing. (1988a: 75)

Or, more lyrically:

> That's just it: the feeling that the impossible is possible. That the necessary is contingent. That linkage must be made, but that there won't be anything upon which to link. The 'and' with nothing to grab onto. Hence not just the contingency of the how of linking, but the vertigo of the last phrase. Absurd, of course. But the lightning flash takes place – it flashes and bursts out of the nothingness of the night, of clouds, or of the clear blue sky. (1988a: 75)

Unfortunately, in *The Differend*, this answer is left hanging, only to be picked up in Lyotard's work on the Kantian sublime and on the artists Macherroni and Newman (although there is a further appeal to the feeling of the sublime, or more precisely, to sublime feelings in *The Differend* but in a context other than the occurrence of phrases). To understand the transition to the later work, note how the above quote on presentation is mirrored in Lyotard's study of the painting of Barnett Newman as sublime in 'Newman: the instant', collected in *The Lyotard Reader*:

> Occurrence is the instant which 'happens', which 'comes' unexpectedly but which, once it is there, takes its place in the network of what has happened. Any instant can be the beginning, provided that it is grasped in terms of its quod rather than its quid. Without this flash, there would be nothing or there would be chaos. The flash (like the instant) is always there and never there. The world never stops beginning. For Newman, creation is not an act performed by someone: it is what happens (this) in the midst of the indeterminate. (Lyotard 1989b: 243)

According to Lyotard, Newman's paintings succeed in presenting something that demands a reaction without having to represent any particular thing (see illustration overleaf). This success can be explained through the feeling of the sublime: the paintings incite a

Barnett Newman, *Adam*, 1951–2

feeling that demands a reaction but leaves no clue as to what the action should be. To do this the content of the painting, what it means, must be preceded by what the painting incites; that is, the feeling happens independent of any realization of meaning.

Perhaps a parallel can be found in the feeling of disquiet we feel sometimes almost out of the blue, due to some apparently insignificant change in the breeze, for example. It is then said that 'someone has trodden on one's shadow', or that 'someone has walked over one's grave' – there has been a premonition of something, but we know not what. The feeling of disquiet far exceeds its minute cause and, prior to any thought on what we have just had a premonition of, we feel that something of import has been announced to us. Thus is Lyotard's feeling of the sublime: 'a feeling of "there" [*Voilà*]. There is almost nothing to "consume", or if there is, I do not know what it is. One cannot consume an occurrence, but merely its meaning' (Lyotard 1989b: 241). For him, everything that happens, every phrase, has the potential to be like Newman's paintings. Every phrase is like the changing breeze, a demand for a reaction, but with no indication of how to react. The demand takes place with the presentation brought forth by a sentence, the reaction takes place with a situation of the initial presentation. This is why Lyotard can base his distinction of presentation and situation on the feeling of the sublime. Every phrase has the potential to demand our attention through the feeling of the sublime, but our explanations of what exactly called for us to react cannot fit the initial feeling.

Lyotard develops this argument from painting to phrases in a little-known interpretation of the paintings of Henri Macherroni, *La Partie de peinture*. The paintings are arranged in series, each painting representing a simple figure, such as a circle or a cross. Lyotard's point is that in a series the paintings appear to be part of a significant structure, where the meaning of an individual painting depends on the series as a whole. But each painting also has an impact independent of the series and there must therefore be an initial event in each painting prior to any concatenation: 'Despite the fact that each figure concatenates with other prior and posterior figures, according to the rules for the formation of series, the secret is that each figure is, not the first figure, but, each time, the only figure' (Lyotard 1980b: 15). Maccheroni's paintings allow Lyotard to make his point about presentation and situation with greater strength. As an individual painting each work brings forth a presentation; this presentation is then only situated as the work is included in a series. The presentation will always exceed its later situation, and this also holds true for phrases:

> [Maccheroni's] idea could be that in the phrase, the most common work of language, lies the secret sought by painting in its most extreme asceticism: to present, and nothing more. And when he directs his plastic art towards language, he is not aiming at the gossip of the combination that cross-multiplies matrices of figures, but at the void from which a phrase

tears, and thanks to which it proposes the worlds it presents for an instant. (1980b: 15)

Although the work on Maccheroni predates *The Differend*, Lyotard had to wait until after that book to unlock the secret of presentation through the feeling of the sublime in the paintings of Barnett Newman. It is interesting, though, to note how the philosopher exploits avant-garde art within a philosophy of language. Perhaps this is what makes Lyotard such a distinctive and exciting thinker: he extends the scope of significant structures into the realm of plastic events, through his understanding of, and feel for, art.

More will be made of this reference to avant-garde art, the final recurrent theme of Lyotard's work, in chapter 6, where the role of the avant-garde and the feeling of the sublime in politics will be explained further. What must be stressed here is the philosophical work Lyotard has had to do in order to link the feeling of the sublime to that which demands attention but which remains beyond representation and understanding. The key is in the conjunction, in the feeling of the sublime, of two contradictory feelings, the one demanding a response, the other indicating a presence beyond our powers of understanding or representation. Lyotard notes this conjunction in earlier formulations of the sublime: in Edmund Burke's *Philosophical Inquiry into the Origin of our Ideas of the Sublime and the Beautiful*, where it involves terror and delight; and in Immanuel Kant's *Critique of Judgement*, where it involves pleasure and pain in the event of an absolutely large object. Both cases balance the impulse to go further, to follow up the feeling of pleasure or delight, to seek it out, and the impulse to draw away from the unknown in terror or pain. Events which are accompanied by the feeling of the sublime will therefore at the same time demand a reaction from us and make the limitations of our powers clear.

This solves Lyotard's dilemma at least to the extent where, if we accept the existence of the feeling of the sublime, there must be events beyond representation that demand reaction. For these events, for the feeling of the sublime, Lyotard's law of concatenation holds true: 'Concatenation is necessary but how to concatenate is not.' Can we say, though, that all phrases have the potential to be accompanied by the feeling of the sublime? After *The Differend*, Lyotard has developed a theory accounting for the paradoxes involved in the main theme of his work, the event. It seems, however, that this is at the price of having to let go of the general claims of his philosophy of language. Not all phrases can be Barnett Newman paintings, just as not all painters can be Barnett Newman:

What distinguishes the work of Newman from the corpus of the 'avant-gardes', and especially from that of American 'abstract expressionism' is not the fact that it is obsessed with the question of time – an obsession shared by many painters – but the fact that it gives an unexpected answer to the question: its answer is that time is in the picture itself. (Lyotard 1991: 240)

Or is this unfair to Lyotard: could any painting catch us unawares and suddenly strike us with the feeling of the sublime?

The methods of libidinal economics

The main methodological problem for the libidinal economy is how to devise a methodology consistent with the unpredictable emergence of intensities on the libidinal band. According to Lyotard, dispositions or structures channel and exploit feelings and desires, but they also limit them and miss something of their original intensity. Lyotard describes this process as one of cooling down, as if the dispositions appear like rock formations at the edge of a lava flow: as the lava cools down, so the rock begins to appear. The problem for Lyotard is that his account of the libidinal economy, and the methods and goals of his political philosophy, must take the form of a structure or disposition. His philosophy comes after the intensities and therefore falls prey to the process of cooling down that any structure depends on.

The first paradox, then, of any methodology operating in the libidinal economy is that when it takes account of intensity, it only does so through dispositions, and hence it only captures a cold, residual intensity. This could be the logical version of the obstacle to be surmounted by Lyotard's methodology in *Libidinal Economy*: how to take account of intensities in structures that are necessarily distanced from them? The practical version of the obstacle comes to light when goals are set with respect to intensities, for example where Lyotard works to undermine certain dispositions because they dampen down the energy of intensities. The practical problem is: if all dispositions necessarily involve the cooling down of intensities, how can Lyotard devise a methodology (and a teleology) that favours some over others?

Lyotard is like a scientist returning from a field trip on Etna: he will never be able to collect or capture the lava flow itself, only the cold rock. This rock was lava, but now it is no longer molten, no longer the intense energy behind the rock formation. Like the cracks and shapes in the rock, its different textures and shades, the methodology and language of the philosopher of libidinal economy depend on perceived fixed differences. These differences do not belong to the lava flow or intensities but to the cooling down process. In the terms of the libidinal economy, intensities emerge on the libidinal band, they then give rise to meaningful signs in figures and dispositions. These signs, although related to the initial intensities, have lost their energy and their ability to emerge freely on to the libidinal band:

> The intense sign which engenders the libidinal body abandons the vast Moebian skin to the signicative sign, the singularity of a passage or a voyage of affects is herded, closed up into a communicable trace. Whether this trace is communicable, or whether this sign is amenable to systematization, or whether the opposition which conceals (but in what space-time?) the irrelevant difference is permanent, all this refers to the duplicity of signs already noted. (Lyotard 1993a: 25)

This passage plots the substitution of intensities, which in themselves have no fixed meaning and depend on no perceivable differences, by systems of signicative signs, carrying meaning and therefore dependent on differences that can be recognized. How would the system work, how would meaning be communicated, if signs could not be told apart? However, the event of intensity is lost once it is set in a structure that allows for meaning; this structure can then be said to channel the energy of intensities: 'what is essential to a structure . . . is that its fixity or consistency, which allows spatio-temporal maintenance of identical denominations between a this and a not-this, work on a pulsionnal movement as would dams, sluices and channels' (Lyotard 1993a: 25). Lyotard's own discourse, when it means something and therefore depends on the reliable repetition of words, on their identity, is such a libidinal disposition. What, then, is the point of his work on intensities, on desires and feelings as events? The philosophy is concerned with the event of intensity in so far as it is different from the sign which comes to replace it in a system or disposition. Yet it appears that Lyotard is caught in a double bind, as he is in the philosophy of language in *The Differend*. Either intensities are lost in dispositions and his own philosophy cannot speak of them. Or intensities can be adequately referred to through signs and his libidinal philosophy is wrong.

The problem is put well, by Lyotard, in his comments on intensities and the unconscious in Freud. The unconscious is structured like a language and the analyst can read symptoms or syndromes as signs in a structure. The problem is, though, that the intensity of singular events in the unconscious is lost to the lesser intensity of signs in a structure:

> The symptom, or at least the syndrome, will be able to be *read*, analysed and reconstituted as a structure, a stable composition of elements; intense passages, tensors, are then no longer singularities, they take on value, as elements, from their continuation, from their opposition, from a metonymy without end. The unconscious is structured like a language, let's speak of it in this way, that's all it *demands*. It is in fact, and is only so when intensities are in decline, when the incandescence of the bar makes way for the glow of what is discriminating, when the dream is exchanged for the dream-narrative, when the traveller has lain down and sold images for an ear which would relieve him of them. (1993a: 27)

It will always be necessary to interpret unique singularities, singular points on the libidinal band, as repeatable signs in a language. The incandescent bar referred to in the quote above is Lyotard's way of describing the state of the libidinal band prior to the cooling down. The bar draws distinctions between things on the libidinal band, but it spins so fast that no distinctions can be recognized, only the energy, the incandescence of the spinning bar. The point Lyotard is making is that when the bar is at full speed and when the intensities are incandescent, singularities on the libidinal band cannot be distinguished from one another according to which side of the bar they fall on. Only when it slows down do differences begin to appear and dispositions begin to allow for the discrimination between what is on one side of the bar and what is on the other. Lyotard's image of the bar allows him to make a seamless connection between significant structures, dependent on recognizable distinctions and hence on a low-speed bar, and emerging intensities, too intense to allow for such distinctions and hence related to the incandescent, high-speed bar.

For example, when a propeller on an aircraft is at full speed it gives the appearance of a disk. At any given time, it is impossible to tell whether a point on the disk is closer to the leading edge or the trailing edge of the propeller. The distinction between the two edges only makes sense when the propeller has slowed down. This is also true of events or intensities on the libidinal band: they can only be distinguished from one another when their energy has been diminished. The strangeness of this image, like the strangeness of the description of the libidinal band, is born of the difficulty Lyotard has in avoiding dispositions, formulations of the emergence of intensities which allow for discrimination. Lyotard's skill lies in giving the reader a sense of intensities at full incandescence in a structure, an account, that can refer to them only through dispositions capturing intensities in their cooled down, significant state. The extent of the problem can be seen when we remark that, at least in theory, it should be possible to determine the relation of any point on the disk to the spinning propeller (if we took a high-speed camera shot, for example): on the libidinal band this possibility does not exist and Lyotard would describe the camera set-up as just one more disposition.

In *Libidinal Economy*, a solution to Lyotard's double bind is made possible by a counter-analysis of dispositions, set-ups or structures. Yes, it is true that dispositions take hold where there is a cooling of intensities, but it is also true that dispositions and structures depend on the energy of intensities. So, in the quote on Freud above, structure, language and the dream-narrative function because they are the aftermath of intensity but also because they are the source of new intensities. To deprive them of all the energy born of intensities would be to render them inoperative: a useless structure, a dead language and a narrative without a story to tell. Lyotard points out that the opposition of event and structure is a false one; what we really have is a duplicitous relation or dependency. A structure can only capture an event imperfectly, but if it does not release a live event, a structure is itself dead. The double bind is therefore also false: structures, language and dispositions cannot help but carry intensity: 'We must first grasp this: signs are not only terms, stages, set in relation and made explicit in a trail of conquest; they *can also* be, indissociably, singular and vain intensities in exodus' (1993a: 50). Dispositions are the place where two processes come together in a duplicitous relation, a double dealing where each process hides what it owes to the other.

Lyotard gives an explanation of this in terms of Freudian drives. Where there is the death drive (death instinct) there must also be a drive towards life (life instinct or Eros) – see Freud in *Beyond the Pleasure Principle*: 'Our speculations have transformed [the opposition of ego instincts and sexual instincts] into one between the life instincts (Eros) and the death instincts' (Freud 1971: 55). Although the desires of the unconscious drive it towards a deathly stability, like the coldness of dispositions, these drives mingle with a counter drive, Eros or libidinal desire, that pushes the unconscious towards novel, life-enhancing instability.

The example Lyotard gives of this duplicity is typical of his particular brand of philosophical political engagement. It surveys the relation between science, thought and politics in an area where great injustices have been committed through the encounter of different worlds. Lyotard notes how European voyages of discovery – with their scientists, collectors and missionaries – headed out of Western Europe in order to label, survey and convert the world at large. He notes how these enterprises became negative set-ups which froze, bottled up or eliminated a richness and a vitality they could not understand. This is the cold drive of those Western dispositions. However, the destruction and loss alone could not have gone on for long, for it would have run itself out as it ran down the new territories. This running down was forestalled by the exploitation of the world at large, where understanding, conversion and classification allowed for a hugely profitable 'trade'. It is only the duplicitous intermingling of discovery, collection and conversion with the formation of empires and the exploitation of the new territories that kept both processes in force. Thus the cold and deathly drive of recording and converting is mingled with the pleasurable and life-enhancing drive of exploitation and trade.

Lyotard assimilates the work of discovery with the work of the sign, that is, what the discoverer seeks to do is understand the strangeness of a new world, and this is done by interpreting its various aspects as signs used to convey new meaning in the languages of science, religion and business. So the work of structures and dispositions is not only a diminishing of intensities through their replacement by repeatable and known signs, it is also the release of new intensities, for example through the spread of trade and empires: 'thus along with this voyage of research and conquest, where the latter is always postponed, comes, indissociably, an intention, an intention to forge a relation, an intention to forge a revenue' (Lyotard 1993a: 45). The whole question of events and intensities, then, has been shifted to questions about structures and the duplicity of structures with respect to intensities. These new questions transfer any perceived opposition of intensities and dispositions to a duplicity of signs and systems of signs, and how they inhibit and release intensities.

Unlike his work in *The Differend*, where Lyotard continues to struggle with the paradox of events through his philosophy of language and his aesthetics of the sublime, his efforts in *Libidinal Economy* are directed straight into the study of systems. So instead of the opposition or 'duality' of presentation and situation, the libidinal economy involves the duplicity of the concealment of intensities within structures or dispositions: 'This effect is not of duality but of duplicity.' A philosophy seeking a philosophical political act within the libidinal economy will have to work with that duplicity, instead of seeking out the pure event:

> This effect is not of duality, but of duplicity. In the 'theoretical order' it will be necessary to proceed in this way, like the duplicitous bar, not through an anxiety over mimeticism or *adequatio*, but because thought itself is libidinal, because what counts is its force (its intensity) and because it is this that it is *necessary* to overlook in words, this interminable worry, this incandescent duplicity. It is therefore necessary that what one thinks can always be assignable to a theoretical ensemble (semantic, formal, it matters little), and shown equally to despair of such an assigna-tion. (Lyotard 1993a: 31)

Any 'advantage' that *Libidinal Economy* holds over *The Differend* can be put down to this shift from duality to duplicity. It allows Lyotard to work in what he calls here the 'theoretical order', the realm of signs and language, without having to admit a necessary failure to repre-sent or understand events (in the quote this worry is expressed as the anxiety over mimeticism or *adequatio*, that is, over the correspondence of signs to events). The solution turns on the presence of intensities within thought and dispositions. Once this has been established, Lyotard's methodology, with respect to the matter at hand of the libidinal economy, will concentrate on the duplicity of signs. It is important to note, though, that Lyotard has not 'proven' this duplic-ity in the way he seeks to demonstrate every step in *The Differend*. Instead, his conclusions depend on specific cases, voyages of discov-ery and semiology (in *Discours, figure*) and on abortive theoretical studies of Freudian drives and linguistic structures (although the study of these is taken much further in *Des Dispositifs pulsionnels, Dérive à partir de Marx et Freud* and *Discours, figure*).

This lack of universal, well-grounded arguments in *Libidinal Economy* has been the focus for critical remarks made by Lyotard from the point of view of his later philosophy of language. In his quasi-autobiography *Peregrinations* and in later prefaces written for the earlier works, Lyotard has called the libidinal economical phi-losophy 'rhetorical' (1988d: 13) and 'metaphysical' (1980a: iii), as if the earlier work were merely a reflection on his mood, prejudices and political aims at the time of writing. This rapid dismissal is somewhat disingenuous. Lyotard rejects the early work in such a way as to deflect attention from the problems it shares with the later work. There are very powerful reasons (and desires) behind the development of *Libidinal Economy* and some of these reasons apply to *The Differend*, however much Lyotard would like to conceal this behind an autobiographical veil. Interestingly enough, this revision exhibits the very duplicity he analyses so convincingly in *Libidinal Economy*. The later remarks diminish the energy of the earlier work, but they do so only to allow the later work to release unhindered as much of its own energy as possible.

The methodology responding to the actual state of society as libidinal economy thus turns on the issue of duplicity. It is this factor in the relation of events and dispositions or set-ups which allows Lyotard to escape the logical paradox of having to present what cannot be presented and the practical problem of a politics of the event. Two key terms develop the idea of duplicity in the libidinal economy: the tensor and dissimulation. The idea of the tensor allows Lyotard to translate events into signs, and hence allows events into the realm of dispositions. The idea of dissimulation explains how this translation functions and allows Lyotard to work on dispositions in terms of tensors. Duplicity involves the mingling of different drives or forces with respect to intensity, a cooling off and a heating up, for example. Lyotard goes on to define the meeting of these different drives as an intensity, that is, a feeling, an affect or a desire. Therefore, because intensities are events, it is correct to say that events take place where different forces or drives meet. This meeting of drives corresponds to the meeting of incompossible figures and dispositions. Each drive involves a figure or disposition that channels and organizes it. Thus the meeting of opposed drives at the intensity implies the meeting of incompossible figures and dispositions. It is important, though, not to impose a model of cause and effect on this conjunction. Events happen at the same time as the meeting of drives, not before and not after – Lyotard's philosophy is not a scientific materialism where the laws of physics and other natural sciences allow for the explanation of all events.

The event, then, has now been defined as a tensor, an intensity which marks the potential intermingling of opposed and different forces or drives at a given point. This point can operate as a sign, for example it could be a proper name: 'Were it necessary to give an example of the way in which the tensor can dissimilate itself in semantics and dissimulate this latter, we could take that of the proper name' (Lyotard 1993a: 55). Thus the proper name 'Nelson Mandela' is a tensor marking the intermingling of the drive towards a South Africa free of apartheid channelled through the political disposition of the ANC, the drive towards white domination channelled through the disposition of apartheid, the desire for a united South Africa and many other potential drives and desires. The use of potential here is to underline, first, how the tensor can be recognized prior to the detection of forces or drives as a potential seat for their mingling and, second, how the number of factors involved is uncertain.

This definition has given Lyotard the opportunity to define the event in the context of dispositions associated with actual and potential desires and drives. It has also allowed Lyotard to maintain events as beyond understanding and representation, through the intensity which drives and desires latch on to or exploit: '[The name] will render compatible a multitude of incompossible propositions concerning the same subject of the statement' (1993a: 55). So a sign as tensor marks the cross-over of intensities and structures: '[the sign is] at the same time a sign which produces meaning through difference and opposition, and a sign producing intensity through force [*puissance*] and singularity' (1993a: 54). Once again, Lyotard's most accessible account of this tensor is in 'Petite économie libidinale d'un dispositif narratif: la régie Renault raconte le meurtre de Pierre Overney' (in 1980a). There, Overney's death is described as a tensor, as a sign remarkable because of the intensity of feelings, desires and affects associated with it, and it is also the potential locus for the meeting of wholly opposed forces: the desire of the Renault factory bosses to cover up the death of a young activist outside their factory, in order to diminish the energy it could release; the militant movement's desire to exploit it in order to increase the energy of their own movement; the desire of others for justice, and so on. In the tensor, recognizable events and signs have become events and intensities in Lyotard's sense.

Now we can see how political events can be understood on his terms, for example in the opposition of forces of outrage and excitation, of entrenchment and suppression, of exhilaration and terror around events such as Bloody Sunday, Sharpeville, the Prague Spring, Tiananmen Square. It is important to note that Lyotard also develops this interest in the proper names of history in the later philosophy, in particular in 'The sign of history', in The Lyotard Reader: 'At the beginning of this lecture, I named certain events which proved a paradoxical, negative occasion for this highly cultivated community sense to reveal itself publicly: Auschwitz, Budapest 1956, May 1968' (1989b: 409). These are, of course, high-profile examples, but this is not what qualifies them as tensors. Any event which is associated with intensity and therefore has the potential to mark the mingling of different forces fits Lyotard's definition. These events need not be catalysts or symbols; in fact, it is equally possible for a tensor to be a general sign within a structure. For example, crime is a tensor marking the different tensions in a society governed by gross economic and social inequalities.

There is a process of dissimulation where particular dispositions are set up to exploit, dissipate and direct the intensities, the energy, associated with a particular tension. Dissimulation describes how the intensity is hidden and altered (Lyotard is playing on the words dissimulate and dissimilate, *dissimuler, dissimiler*) in the disposition. Thus, in the Overney example, the Renault management seek to hide and alter the intensity in the press releases handed out after the event. These press releases are narrative dispositions: dispositions set up to channel the desire to cover up the events through a narrative of what happened. It is not too difficult to see this process at work in modern media management, as press officers, spin doctors and communication officers seek to manipulate intensities in favour of their interest group, politician or product. They do this by taking the name or sign associated with the intensity and by developing an account around that name in the direction of different forces or desires. The signs of a nation, the flag and the anthem, bring together many different and opposed desires and ideas of nationhood. Marketing firms will seek to pull the intensity of the sign or tensor in the direction of their client. This is the power of marketing in capitalism, to exploit the tensors within society in the release and transferral of energy from set-up to set-up. These accounts therefore dissimulate and dissimilate the intensity, they hide it and alter it within the account:

> Let us be content to recognize in dissimulation all that we have been seeking, difference within identity, the chance event within the foresight of composition, passion within reason – between each, so absolutely foreign to each other, the strictest unity: dissimulation. (Lyotard 1993a: 52)

However, unlike the restricted advocacy for one or other specific intensity (in sexual liberation, for example), Lyotard's aim will be to encourage all intensities through dissimulation, not favouring one desire over all others. This inscription of intensity within dispositions is what will interest Lyotard in his development of the political philosophical act. It is there that the event and the power of feelings can be found in structures. It is also there, or through this process, that structures can be undermined and hijacked, because the dissimulation of intensity within a disposition must also involve the dissimulation of other potential drives and forces. Therefore, other potential dispositions can be recognized within the initial one.

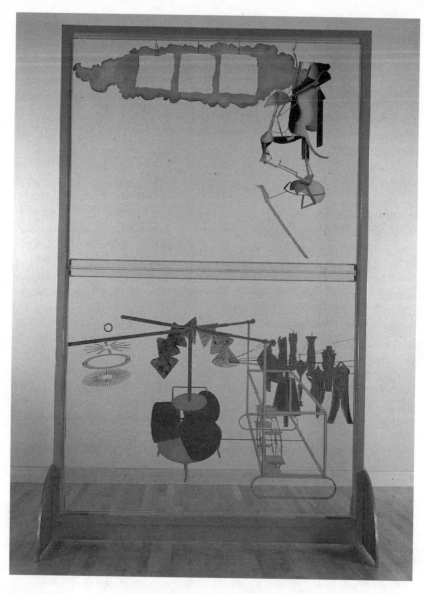

Marcel Duchamp, *Large Glass,* **1967**
Tate Gallery, London. © ADAGP, Paris and DACS, London 1998.

In the following quote, the Christian disposition is shown to conceal and alter the figure of the antichrist in the figure of Christ, this dissimulation marking the encounter and intertwining of the Christian disposition and heretical dispositions. To support the argument put forward in the passage, Lyotard could call on the many examples of hereticism from the history of Christianity – in particular, the dissimulation of sex in love and love in sex has played many tricks:

> Thus the Antichrist preaching in the square painted by Signorelli in an Orvieto fresco is exactly like Christ, so it is true that Christ *dissimulates* the Antichrist in the sense that he conceals his fearsome mission from the latter in his speeches, and when he says 'love one another', it would take very little for the most disastrous misunderstanding to ensue (and in fact it does); and the Antichrist dissimulates Christ in so far as he simulates the latter, as close to him as makes no difference, this being the *'dis-'* of dissimulation, or dissimilation. (1993a: 52)

At first, it appears quite strange for Lyotard to take the side of dissimulation, of hidden and altered intensities. This makes sense, however, when we remember that this is an alternative to the rejection of intensities out of dispositions and set-ups. Lyotard's teleology, the development of his philosophical and political aims, will be able use the terms tensor and dissimulation to solve the problem of how to develop aims that take account of the unpredictable emergence of intensities on the libidinal band. Again, Lyotard applies his work on dispositions and dissimulation to an example from modern art. In *Les Transformateurs Duchamp*, the work studied by him is Duchamp and Hamilton's *Large Glass* (see illustration): '[Duchamp's] mechanism dissimulates, it does not belong to the things of power, to politics, to technic. It is the mechanism of machination' (Lyotard 1977: 62). It is worth noting the contrast between Duchamp's work and the paintings of Barnett Newman: what this contrast shows is the move from complex dissimulations of intensities, desires and feelings, within dispositions, into the association of an event beyond representation and the feeling of the sublime.

Conclusion

Though Lyotard's philosophy develops some of the most important and interesting intuitions concerning the postmodern condition and the possibility of irresolvable conflicts, his methodological arguments for the truth of those intuitions are often incomplete and sometimes inconsistent. As we have seen, his philosophy of language stretches the definition of phrase, regimen and genre to breaking point, that is, we must either accept the wide definition of phrase and reject its connection to an analysis of specific phrase regimens or turn to a more narrow definition of phrase and lose its connection to Lyotard's definition of the event. So it appears that he cannot resolve the problems and paradoxes raised by his description of the postmodern condition by appealing to a set of loosely related linguistic properties, such as rigid designation, for example. Indeed, in Lyotard's work on the sublime, the philosophy of language gives way to an aesthetics where we are no longer concerned with sense and reference but with feelings and the sensible. This turn to art and aesthetics returns Lyotard to earlier arguments developed in *Discours, figure* and *Libidinal Economy*.

However, even if we accept the ultimate failure of the philosophy of language in terms of Lyotard's aims concerning the event and the differend, this does not mean that his aesthetics holds more promise in terms of decisive arguments for his long-held intuitions. On the contrary, *Libidinal Economy* explicitly rejects traditional forms of philosophical argument in favour of a strategy of provocation through subversion. The theoretical connections drawn up in *Libidinal Economy* come to rest on definitions of duplicity and dissimulation that complicate the pure theoretical terms of tensor and disposition. Here, complication must take on a negative sense from the point of view of the search for rational arguments, since dissimulation and duplicity depend on the successful release of intensity defined as passion or emotion. We must 'feel' that the theory is true; indeed, the strength of the feelings released is the only test of the validity of the theory. Lyotard's libidinal economy is a double provocation in the sense that it is ultimately put forward against deduction or evidence and that it undermines its own status as theory. The reader must be carried away by the force of this alliance of rhetoric and theory, or must simply turn away. A narrowly defined rational approach, seeking out a well-grounded and logically consistent philosophy, is ultimately pushed to the second option.

6

Politics

Political acts

The basis for the goals of Lyotard's philosophy, the specific acts and
the overall aim of the political act, lies in the uncontrolled and
unpredictable emergence of feelings and desires driving the philosopher to act. These feelings and desires emerge either as libidinal
desires, in the context of the libidinal economy, or as the feeling of
the sublime, in the context of the postmodern condition. They are
therefore consistent with Lyotard's descriptions of the actual state of
society and with the methodologies applicable to them. What distinguishes these feelings and desires from others, in terms of acts, is
their association with the event, with intensities and with absolute
differences. A first understanding of acts in Lyotard's philosophy
could be that they are based on feelings and desires that are sensitive to, and attracted to, events beyond understanding, to absolute
differences and to intense feelings and desires.

It is worth noting two things here. First, Lyotard's position contrasts with the prevalent search for mediation in philosophical politics. Second, his politics has an aesthetic basis as opposed to a
scientific one. The second point will be tackled later in terms of
Lyotard's development of the theme of the avant-garde. The first
point follows from a view of the philosopher as a wise and knowl-
edgeable mediator in politics. The philosopher can be seen as a
political agent whose knowledge, wisdom and powers of thought
allow for the reconciliation of conflicting views according to deeper
truths. Lyotard's position contradicts this through the affirmation of

conflicts that are beyond resolution and through the defence of events and intensities that exceed any powers of wisdom or knowledge. Lyotard's political philosophy is important because he provides a counterbalance to the goal of mediation; he shows the danger of the desire to resolve conflicts once and for all.

Lyotard's teleology, in the case of the libidinal economy, will involve a desire to act in such a way as to allow intensities to occur, that is, to release energy from systems that capture and inhibit it. This does not mean to make them occur, for this is impossible. There is no relation of cause and effect between intensities and dispositions or set-ups, the structures in which acts must be developed. It means to act in such a way as to allow for the possibility of the emergence of intensities. The key to this encouragement lies in the idea of dissimulation, the concealment and alteration of intensities in dispositions. There must be a way of acting that undermines systems by surreptitiously releasing the energy that they exploit and capture. However, if acts in the libidinal economy are planned and executed solely according to systems and theory, then they set up and depend on dispositions. This means that the only way in which a drive towards or a desire for intensities can succeed is through acts which dissimulate intensities within dispositions, that is, acts which allow signs in structures to become events associated with the emergence of a libidinal event. The philosopher is like an undercover agent, 'no politics, rather a conspiracy' (Lyotard 1993a: 42).

In a libidinal politics, communication must be double edged. The philosopher, like the agent, must seek ways of dissimulating signs which can release intensity. This is because the philosopher has no direct access to intensities: any act takes place in a disposition. Therefore the main aim will be set by the desire for intensities, a desire for libidinal events. The particular goals linked to this main aim will be acts which allow for the dissimulation of events in set-ups, that is, the dissimulation of tensors as signs in dispositions: 'Let us be content to recognize in dissimulation all that we have been seeking, difference within identity, the chance event within the foresight of composition, passion within reason' (1993a: 52). This work of concealment and alteration will be entirely dependent on the dispositions or set-ups in which it must take place. There is no one way to dissimulate. Perhaps a useful parallel here is camouflage. Something is not concealed in the desert in the same way as in the Arctic or the tropical jungle. So philosophical political acts in the libidinal economy are extremely varied. This is a result of the need for them to take account of the particular dispositions in which they have to take place. What they do share, though, is a desire to let intensities happen.

The postmodern condition provides a very different basis for action than the libidinal economy. First of all, in the postmodern condition, priority is given to the feeling of the sublime associated with the presentation brought forth by a phrase, that is, the feeling associated with events. This feeling brings together an impulse to act and the feeling that no action is the correct one. It is necessary to follow a given phrase or a given event but there is no correct way of doing this. Here, the feeling of the sublime drives the philosopher to bear witness to what is associated with the feeling, that is, to search for ways of speaking for an event. This witnessing will be the basis for action. The commitment involves two specific acts as its goals: to bear witness to events and to bear witness to differences that cannot be resolved. The first act will seek to awaken others to the possibility of events, that is, to things that occur but that are beyond representation and understanding. According to Lyotard's philosophy of language this will be to awaken others to the law of concatenation, 'To link is necessary but a particular linkage is not.' Things occur, they demand judgement, decisions, reactions, but there is no correct way of following on from those occurrences. What we can do is bear witness to this fact. Lyotard calls this bearing witness to the differend, that is, to bear witness to the absolute difference between events in general and our representations and understanding of them.

There is, though, a severe problem with this approach. It appears to leave Lyotard, the philosopher of political commitment, in an awkward dead-end. If there is no correct link or way of following on from an event, then the philosopher has no correct actions other than to bear witness to this problem. What, then, is the point of bearing witness in the first place?

The solution is to take account of a further consequence of events or the law of concatenation: incommensurable language games or genres. The incommensurability of language games or genres is a result of the occurrence of events and of Lyotard's law of concatenation. What this means is that ways of judging, reacting to, or following on from events have no common measure. It is possible for different practices to be equally justified in their ways of linking on to events, or to phrases. When two such practices, governed by the rules of incommensurable genres or language games, come to dispute the same event, an irresolvable conflict arises. That is, a conflict occurs that cannot be resolved justly from the point of view of both practices. Lyotard calls this conflict a differend, although here it will be a specific differend as opposed to the differend in general. These differends – note the plural in this case, as opposed to the singular in the case of the differend in general – can also be borne witness to. This will be the postmodern political task: 'What is at stake in a literature, in a philosophy, in a politics perhaps, is to bear witness to differends by finding idioms for them' (Lyotard 1988a: 13).

Again, these specific differends come to light through feelings and the task of bearing witness to them must involve a recourse to forms that are not implicated in the differend. Lyotard calls these novel forms new idioms, and they are necessary because any appeal to a form already involved in the differend would involve a taking of sides; this would be to ignore the irresolvable nature of the conflict, that is, it would be to prolong the differend instead of testifying to it.

Testifying to the differend

Lyotard begins *The Differend* with a consideration of specific cases of conflicts that require judgement. What distinguishes these cases from others is the desperate position in which they put the plaintiffs, those who bring the case to court. There seems to be no way of putting their case to the satisfaction of the court, that is, the court demands a testimony which cannot be given, due to the nature of the wrong done to the plaintiffs. The case is therefore rejected and the wrong cannot be rectified. Lyotard then says that the plaintiff has become a victim: 'It is in the nature of a victim not to be able to prove that one has been done a wrong. A plaintiff is someone who has incurred damages and who disposes of the means to prove it. One becomes a victim if one loses these means' (Lyotard 1988a: 8). The position is desperate because the transformation of the plaintiff into a victim is inevitable in the particular court. This inevitability stems from the conflict between the form of argumentation accept-able to the court and the form of argumentation required by the plaintiff to put the case: 'I would call a *differend* the case where the plaintiff is divested of the means to argue and becomes for that reason a victim' (1988a: 9).

Such cases can take place, Lyotard argues, when a plaintiff is asked to present a case in a language which nullifies it. The plaintiff is asked to perform a self-defeating task where the form of evidence demanded by the court cannot be given. Examples of these instances could be: to have to prove rape in a language and culture that has no conception of what this could be; to be asked to give an example of a great event that has not yet been publicized, when wide public acclaim is a necessary condition for greatness; to be asked to provide physical evidence of the absolute destruction of something. In all these cases the victim is reduced to silence by the demands of the court: 'The differend is signalled by this inability to prove. The one who lodges the complaint is heard, but the one who is a victim, and who is perhaps the same one, is reduced to silence'(1988a: 10).

In the terminology of the postmodern condition, differends arise out of the conflicts of incommensurable language games. A wrong can be suffered but also judged justly, in a language game, when the game provides the framework for expressing or understanding that wrong. However, it is also possible for the same wrong to have to be judged from within another game incommensurable to the prior one. This second game will not have the framework necessary for the equitable judgement of the wrong. In the latter case, the wrong becomes a differend. Differends occur where a court operates according to a language game incommensurable with the language game of the plaintiff. For example, there could be the language game of human rights, asserting that every person has a right to a fair trial, and the language game of reasons of state, when a state is up against terrorism, for instance. Where the state judges itself to be in such great danger as to warrant dropping a commitment to human rights and where it then acts against terrorists in such a way as to deny them a right to a fair trial, there is a differend. The state passes judgement – an internment policy, for example – according to a language game incommensurable with the language game of human rights. The victims of internment cannot prove their innocence because the state refuses to disclose the reasons behind its judgement, 'for reasons of state'. This legal treatment of the differend provides the first opportunity for action within the postmodern condition. Society involves the conflicts of incommensurable language games. These conflicts give rise to differends. It is the task of the philosopher to bear witness to them.

Lyotard's teleology depends on an assessment of the postmodern condition and on the development of a strategy for action. The result of the assessment is, first, to isolate legal differends as the locus for the greatest injustice in society and, second, to decide to act by bearing witness to this injustice. The steps are at their most clear in Lyotard's *Au Juste* (1979) where he goes into the question of justice in the context of differences that cannot be resolved. Literally, *au juste* means 'exactly', in terms of the exact judgement of measure or value. This is inappropriately translated as 'just gaming' in the English translation of the book, thereby losing the sense of a search for a just measure in favour of a playful conception of language games. However, these steps alone are insufficient for the development of a teleology: there remain the questions of how to recognize differends and how to bear witness to them. These questions are far from trivial. In a differend there is, on the one hand, a wrong that cannot be expressed and, on the other hand, a system of judgement that cannot see the wrong. If the philosopher operates within the language of the first, then there will be no way of expressing the wrong in the language of the second. If the philosopher operates in the language of the second, then there will be no way of recognizing the wrong. Once again, Lyotard has drawn us into a double bind.

But surely the solution to the double bind is to operate in a language independent of the two sides in the differend? This is indeed the case, because otherwise the philosopher either has to be a victim or an unjust judge. However, this 'solution' brings in problems of its own. Lyotard has characterized the differend as an irresolvable conflict, which means there can be no judgement that brings both sides together while remaining consistent with their original claims. Thus the political role of the philosopher cannot be to resolve the conflict in favour of one side or the other, because this would be to perpetrate an injustice on the other side. Neither can the philosopher resolve the conflict to the satisfaction of both sides – their positions are beyond reconciliation. Instead, the philosophical political act will be to show that the two sides cannot be brought together and this will be to testify to the differend.

The political function of testimony is unproblematic where a clear and just settlement is available. However, there can be no such settlement within the parameters of the differend and any such mediation or resolution will prolong or modify it. There are many examples of these misguided attempts in the history of borders and states. To draw compromise borders, to institute umbrella states and to rectify a great wrong through the creation of new homelands is often to shift the original conflict underground, to store it up for later and to transfer it to a different age or to different protagonists. Worse, this reconciliation sometimes hides another programme, that is, a knowledge that the conflict remains but that this is a price worth paying in a wider or narrower context. Such concealment can be a conscious plan or merely a failure to sense the differend. So the postmodern political act cannot seek a resolution; instead, it must find ways of expressing the differend as an irresolvable conflict. Where there is a feeling that something must be done and where that feeling accompanies a conflict beyond resolution, the task must be to encourage the sides to change by awakening them to the depth of their conflict: to testify to their differend as irresolvable.

In Lyotard's politics something has to be made of nothing or, at least, of a senseless opposition. However, how can an absolute opposition be recognized and how can it be testified to? He answers this question by translating it into his philosophy of language. Differends are conflicts between incommensurable genres or language games. A phrase occurs and two incommensurable genres enter into dispute over the right way to concatenate on from the initial phrase. The law of concatenation dictates that there is no correct way of linking on to the initial phrase and the genres are therefore incommensurable with respect to the phrase. The dispute between the two genres as to how to concatenate is then a differend. In the legal terminology from above, an event occurs, and for one party this event is the site of a wrong, for another party it is not. It is impossible for the two parties to reconcile their differences because their accounts belong to different genres; therefore, they form two sides of a differend.

Once Lyotard has translated the legal differend into his philosophy of language, he is in a position to apply the answers from the philosophy to the problems of the legal differend. The incommensurability of language games is deduced from the feeling of the sublime which accompanies the presentation brought forth by a phrase. Similarly, an absolute difference, a conflict that cannot be resolved, is associated with the feeling of the sublime, the contrary conjunction of pleasure and pain, delight and terror. The pain or terror is associated with the sheer desperation of the conflict. The pleasure or delight is associated with the creative effort to express the differend where differences must be drawn out in a form free of the initial opposition:

> This is when the human beings who thought they could use language as an instrument of communication learn through the feeling of pain which accompanies silence (and of pleasure which accompanies the invention of a new idiom) that they are summoned by language, not to augment to their profit the quantity of information communicable through existing idioms, but to recognize that what remains to be phrased exceeds what they can presently phrase, and that they must be allowed to institute new idioms which do not yet exist. (Lyotard 1988a: 13)

The feeling of the sublime is not the basis for a resolution of conflicts – on the contrary, it draws attention to absolute differences. In addition to this, the feeling brings the differend in general to the fore, for example in the way Lyotard uses it to justify his idea of presentation. This second, general, aspect allows the sublime to emphasize the constant possibility of events. In fact, no resolution of a conflict, no act at all, is free of the occurrence of events. That is, any act has the potential to lead to differends. So the feeling of the sublime has a double action: it is associated with the differend in particular and the differend in general. This is critical, because without the possibility of further differends it will always be possible to sacrifice any particular differend in the name of a utopic state, a state where the differend has been eliminated. Lyotard's philosophy does not allow for this utopic illusion; in this, he escapes the philosophical goal of an ultimate reconciliation and he avoids the totalitarian dream of eliminating conflict through the eradication or management of differences.

The fact remains, though, that the feeling of the sublime is not in itself an act. It is not enough to argue in favour of the feeling if there is not also at least a gesture as to how to act once the sublime has revealed the differend. Without such a gesture, Lyotard will be restricted to a frustrating nihilism: 'there are irresolvable conflicts but there is nothing we can do about them.' Yet Lyotard does speak of the institution of new idioms as a positive way of testifying to the differend. How is this to be done? Any answer to the question must take account of two points: first, Lyotard does not develop an answer of his own in *The Differend*; this is a surprising lack in the light of the injunction to testify to the differend. Second, any answer must take account of a series of severe obstacles to acts based on the differend or the conflict between incommensurable genres. In particular, the act must not involve a taking of sides, for this would be to reinforce the differend. The act must not put forward a resolution to the conflict – there can be no such thing. The act can offer no guarantees as to its outcome because it is itself an event. We must bear witness in a form independent of any of the forms of expression and judgement already involved in the differend. We must avoid the illusion of providing a solution to the conflict; instead, we must convey the irresolvable nature of differends.

Lyotard's act of testifying to the differend through the institution of new idioms is a response to these limitations. To testify to the differend is not to put forward a resolution of the conflict, but to develop a novel mode of expression for the absolute differences separating the two sides. The institution of new idioms avoids the danger of expressing the conflict within the idiom of one of the sides and so failing to bring out the differend. What is more, the act of testifying to a differend also displays its own status as an event by bringing attention to the differend in general.

A development of Lyotard's ideas on testimony can be found in his work on avant-garde art, in particular in the essays 'The sublime and the avant-garde' and 'Newman: the instant' (both in *The Inhuman: Reflections on Time*, 1991). Lyotard develops a distinctive definition of avant-garde art as the art form dedicated to the feeling of the sublime and, through the feeling, to particular differends and to the differend in general. Lyotard draws on the ability of avant-garde artists to institute radical change within an art form. He is interested in changes that set off new artistic techniques, new ways of thinking about art and, ultimately, new ways of thinking about events. The connection of the avant-garde to the sublime allows Lyotard to exploit the practical example of avant-garde art. It can be a practice that breaks aesthetic and critical rules, emphasizing the association of the feeling of the sublime with the differend. In this way, the act sought in relation to the differend becomes a possibility. The avant-garde is the key to the necessary suspension of established forms of judgement and understanding involved in the act, while the feeling of the sublime is the key to an effective testimony that does not allow for a resolution. The avant-garde attempts to produce art outside established rules of art production.

The act of testifying to the differend must resemble the creative act of avant-garde art, because the former requires the same invention of new rules – 'new idioms' – as the latter. The feeling of the sublime allows for a testimony free of the possibility of a resolution, through the conjunction of contradictory feelings, pleasure and pain or delight and terror. Pleasure accompanies the search for a new idiom but the pain accompanies the realization that there can never be a resolution within the existing idiom. This contradiction maintains the act of testimony as something that awakens us to a conflict but that also awakens us to the impossibility of resolving the conflict. We are then aware of a differend and of the differend.

This connection of the avant-garde and the sublime is all-important. Lyotard brings our attention to the shock and doubt caused by avant-garde art as rules and conventions are broken. In effect, the art form, in order to bring about new feelings and thoughts, goes beyond the established ways we have for thinking through and judging the art work. The history of twentieth-century art has been a succession of revolutions and innovations that have broken the rules and conventions of prior artistic practices and values. These revolutions in art have often run parallel and born witness to the events of the century in a way that the art forms immediately prior to them could not have done (Picasso's *Guernica*, for instance). What Lyotard shows is why this connection holds. The break with established taste and critical measures allows for the eruption of new feelings and thoughts. These feelings and thoughts could not have taken place within the established ways. The shock of avant-garde art 'dismantles consciousness' and 'exceeds understanding' and yet it captures our attention through our feelings: something new must be thought through here.

In parallel to the conjunction of pleasure and pain in the act of creation there is a similar clash in the emotions of the spectator. Avant-garde art involves the contrary feelings of shock or doubt, as our established ways crumble, and attraction or pleasure, at the expression of something new, of new possibilities. Each avant-garde work is an occasion for the feeling of the sublime, 'bearing pictorial or otherwise expressive witness to the inexpressible':

> Here and now there is this painting, rather than nothing, and that's what is sublime. Letting go of all grasping intelligence and of its power, disarming it, recognizing that this occurrence of painting was not necessary and is scarcely foreseeable, a privation in the face of *Is it happening?* guarding the occurrence 'before' any defence, any illustration, and any commentary, guarding before being on one's guard, before 'looking' (*regarder*) under the aegis of now, this is the rigour of the avant-garde. (Lyotard 1991: 199)

The 'privation in the face of *Is it happening?*' refers to the effect of being stripped of one's cognitive faculties. This happens before we know what is happening. Note how the account offers a way of explaining the idea of the presentation brought forth by a phrase from Lyotard's philosophy of language. The presentation exceeds any subsequent situations in the same way as the work of art exceeds any established aesthetic criteria.

Lyotard has often put his extensive knowledge of modern art to work in his philosophy; he has also put his philosophy to work in the critical definition of modern art. The dual relation is a highly fruitful one; it allows him to exploit the feelings, affects and desires experienced in art within the field of philosophy, thereby resolving the problem of how to act with respect to feelings and desires. It also allows him to release the power of works of art in the critical and conceptual fields by giving them a critical and conceptual back-ground taken from philosophy. An example of this interrelationship could be found in the exhibition *Les Immatériaux*, of which Lyotard was the curator, at the Centre Georges Pompidou in Paris (see the catalogue to this exhibition, Lyotard 1985b). Further examples can be found in his books on artists such as Marcel Duchamp (*Les Transformateurs Duchamp*). In the following passage, for instance, Lyotard draws a parallel between his philosophical work on incom-mensurability and Duchamp's contrary and disturbing avant-garde works: 'But could it be that M. Duchamp has sought for and ob-tained, or Mme Sélavy has sought for and obtained, *contrariety* in terms of space and time and of matter and form? Or do you prefer to say *incommensurability*?' (1977: 13).

In the case of the definition of the avant-garde in terms of the sublime, Lyotard is able to avoid the disintegration of the avant-garde into worthless innovation by insisting that avant-garde art must be sublime. In this way, avant-garde art is saved from a definition dependent on the market, that is, the definition of the avant-garde as innovative works that people will buy merely be-cause they are shockingly different. The shock of the sublime is more precise. It combines pain with pleasure, that is, with the sense that something new and worthwhile is occurring. It also requires that the work of art bear testimony to differends and to that which cannot be said. A vague iconoclastic gesture is not enough. Yet innovation is necessary because once works of art become part of established schools and once they become understood in terms of known critical values, they will be in danger of losing their ability to shock and their ability to exceed our cognitive faculties. This loss leads to an inability to testify to the differend through the feeling of the sublime.

Lyotard's discussion of avant-garde art and the sublime adds sub-tlety to the discussion on modern and postmodern art. At times, the distinction drawn between modern and postmodern art has taken on a political significance around the opposition of modernist enlighten-ment and postmodernist conservatism. For example, in his *What's Wrong with Postmodernism*, Christopher Norris argues that although Lyotard is sensitive to contemporary political problems his work on the sublime precludes any meaningful political action: 'Worst of all, these ideas deprive critical thought of the one resource most needful at present, i.e. the competence to judge between good and bad argu-ments, reason and rhetoric, truth-seeking discourse and the "postmodern" discourse of mass-induced media stimulation' (1990:

44). For Norris, Lyotard's 'modish aesthetic ideology' (p.45) is necessarily reactionary because it cannot provide a way forward on the basis of its definition of testimony, in art or otherwise.

However, what we learn from the discussion on the sublime and the avant-garde is that the simplistic political opposition does not fit the aesthetic discussion, at least where Lyotard is concerned. His definition of the avant-garde is not conservative, in the sense of incapable of reforming or revolutionary actions. On the contrary, it advocates a creative break free of any nostalgia for absolute forms or values. So although modern and postmodern works have been described as avant-garde, only the postmodern works are sublime, because they do not maintain the possibility of a time without breaks and events. Lyotard makes this point in the essay 'What is postmodernism?' in *The Postmodern Condition*: 'The postmodern would be that which, in the modern, puts forward the unpresentable in presentation itself; that which denied itself the solace of good forms ...' (1984b: 81). If Lyotard's philosophy is to be labelled conservative, the point cannot be on the basis of a collusion with 'mass-induced media stimulation'. His idea of a postmodern political act, as the first point in any modern movement, is exactly to break with comfortable and comforting simulations, including a facile resort to shock.

Avant-garde art allied to the sublime offers the philosopher of action a model of how to testify to differends and to the differend. More significantly perhaps, each avant-garde work of art offers an individual model of how to testify. In order to remain sensitive to that individuality, Lyotard's texts on works of art are somewhat removed from his philosophical work. This is because each text grasps an opportunity to follow on from an event that releases feelings and intensities: the work of art. For example, the texts on Valerio Adami, Ruth Franken and Barnett Newman ('Anamnesis of the visible, or candour', 'Newman: the instant' and 'The Story of Ruth', in *The Lyotard Reader*) are highly individual attempts to link on from the works of those particular artists.

However, these acts can be drawn together by a series of points on how to testify to a differend:

1 To testify to a differend an act must arouse the feeling of the sublime.
2 The feeling of the sublime involves a disturbance of settled ways of understanding; the act must therefore involve a break with those ways.

3   The feeling also involves the sense of an opening on to possi-
    bilities; the act must lead to questions rather than give an-
    swers.

If these points are followed, the act will also testify to the differend
in general, that is, to the status of all acts as events. Again, this takes
place through the feeling of the sublime. Those who have to follow
the act become aware of its status as an event and hence they
become aware of the possibility of events. To understand this passage from a differend to the differend, it is important to refer back to
Lyotard's philosophy of language. There the presentation brought
forth by a phrase is the condition for the incommensurability of
genres. In the case of an act that testifies to a differend, the act must
itself be an event and will therefore awaken those who have to
follow the act to the possibility of events in general. However, the
points made above are not easy or automatic to apply: because of the
break with established rules each act will be an experiment, a new
move whose success cannot be predicted. There is no relation of
cause and effect between certain types of act and the feeling of the
sublime.

Dissimulation in the libidinal economy

Many parallels can be drawn between Lyotard's libidinal philosophy and his philosophy of differends. However, any emerging pattern of shared themes and concerns is broken once the politics of
the libidinal economy and the politics of the postmodern condition
come into consideration. This divergence of the two philosophies
has repercussions for any study that insists on their closeness. They
may appear to have much in common, but once their political acts
come into the picture, a great divide opens up. Specifically, though
the two philosophies have ultimate goals relating to events, they
differ in their approach to those goals. In the case of the philosophy
of differends, the event is the condition for any differend, in the
same way as the occurrence of a phrase is the condition for the
incommensurability of genres. Therefore, when Lyotard develops
an act to show the differend he does so in terms of the relation
between the feeling of the sublime and the event and not in terms of
each particular differend. The conjunction of the avant-garde and
the sublime allows Lyotard to bring our attention to the event and
hence only to the differend or to the incommensurability of lan-

guage games. This means that the philosophy finds itself moving away from the differend as such and towards the sublime event. To testify to the differend is to move outside towards the event and towards a privileged feeling.

In the case of the libidinal philosophy, intensities (feelings and desires) are events that cannot be separated from specific conflicts. Names, defined as tensors, conceal intensities and always belong to conflicting narratives or dispositions. They always mark the tension between narratives or dispositions that cannot be reconciled and this is why intensities are associated with them. New intensities must emerge with new tensors, new conflicts of dispositions. In the libidinal economy, there is no outside to turn to: all intensities or events are concealed and generated within conflicting dispositions. The desire of the libidinal philosopher to encourage the emergence of intensities must therefore turn to acts in dispositions. The aim must be to 'set dissimulations to work on behalf of intensities' (Lyotard 1993a: 262). The scale of the difference comes to light here. On the one hand, there is a politics of testimony to the outside, to the event. On the other hand, there is the politics of conspiracy, an effort to undermine from within by releasing or 'conducting' intensities.

However, the libidinal economy and the philosophy of differends still share a fleeting politics, that is, a politics in a constant state of flux with no fixed programme or set of values. This flux is a necessary aspect of a philosophy favouring events, because any positively de-fined philosophy involves an illegitimate knowledge of events. If a philosophy sets down a specific programme or course of action, then the positive nature of the setting down depends on a denial of the possibility of changing circumstances. The event is an absolutely unpredictable occurrence going beyond any programmes that happen to be in place at any given time. Lyotard ensures the fleeting nature of his politics by leaving it to be determined by the practical situations which it has to be applied to. In the philosophy of differends, this means having to adapt to the particular differend involved in a specific conflict between genres. In the case of the libidinal philosophy, this will mean having to work within a given disposition or set of dispositions. Either way, the acts involved in the philosophies are driven by circumstances outside their control. What is more, these acts must deny themselves as bases for any positive political programme: 'You can't make a political "program" with [an occurrence], but you can bear witness to it' (Lyotard 1988a: 181); 'Our politics is of flight, primarily, like our style' (Lyotard 1993a: 20).

But in its politics of flight, *Libidinal Economy* cannot turn to the sublime. The libidinal philosophy does not allow for the singling out of particular feelings in terms of their association with intensities or events. Instead, the libidinal economy involves a multiplicity of duplicitous desires, where duplicity indicates the participation of all desires in conflicting dispositions. It is not possible to have a pure 'sublime feeling' for the event in the libidinal economy; rather, the event is the condition for all intense feelings and desires. The political act cannot then be to testify to the differend or to the event through a privileged feeling. It must be to work for the release of all feelings and desires within dispositions. So, unlike *The Differend*, there is no move to escape an intolerable situation in *Libidinal Economy*. Rather, any situation involves an opportunity to exploit feelings and desires that are already present: 'Let us be content to recognize in dissimulation all that we have been seeking, difference within identity, the chance event within the foresight of composition, passion within reason – between each, so absolutely foreign to each other, the strictest unity: dissimulation' (Lyotard 1993a: 52).

Dissimulation, the concealment and generation of intensities within dispositions, allows for a twofold political act. First, it is to detect and bring to the fore the patterns of dissimulation present in given dispositions. What conflicts are hidden within a given system? Where do they participate in other conflicting systems? Second, it is to set off new patterns of dissimulation. How can new conflicts and hence intensities be allowed to emerge? How can feelings and desires be allowed to proliferate? The study of dissimulation cannot reveal intensities as such; rather, dissimulation involves tensors which dissimulate or are the signs of intensities. So tensors are signs within the dispositions or structures. They mark the meeting of incompossible dispositions and figures. Perhaps more importantly, though, tensors mark the tension between duplicitous forces, like the tension between the Freudian death drive and Eros. One force or drive dissimulates another, 'This machinery does not obey either death or Eros, but both, and is erotic so far as it is an orderly machine (whose discourse will try to produce a rational simulacrum in the texts of Freud or Lacan), and lethal in so far as it is a machine with a fault (which the analyst wishes to repair)' (1993a: 53). The libidinal economist seeks out and creates tensors, turns names into sites of conflict and allows feelings and desires to emerge and be hidden again.

It could never be enough, though, merely to uncover duplicity, because this would be to deny the operation of duplicity in the philosophical political act itself. Libidinal philosophers cannot merely reveal, or criticize, or deconstruct; they must operate according to the processes of the libidinal economy. Their desire for intensities is not merely restricted to the negative acts of uncovering and detection; such neutral acts cannot actually take place in the libidinal economy. Each tracking down of dissimulation must itself dissimulate. Intertwined with the act of detection, in libidinal studies of dispositions there must also be an act of dissimulation. Libidinal economists will seek to dissimulate tensors within systems in the hope of releasing intensities, of encouraging feelings and desires. For example, Lyotard's own book reveals the libidinal economy, but it also conceals desires and feelings in tensors of its own:

> an idea on fire, an image, the smell of a tear gas grenade or an intolerable denial of justice, a face, a book, a tensor sign we had to act on, conducting it and letting it course through a few quick pages, rapidly arranging words into sentences and paragraphs, so that this heat and this chill, this force may pass through. (1993a: 260)

This other side of the philosophical political act in the libidinal economy is to let intensities happen within systems or dispositions by concealing tensors within them. Here it is possible to see the conspiratorial power of libidinal economy. It does not hark to an outside, to an ideal or utopia; rather, it encourages conflict and tension. It is possible, therefore, to act politically according to the libidinal philosophy in any system, or more precisely, anywhere on the libidinal band. This act will involve the study of the system in terms of dissimulation: what tensors are at work here? But it will also involve the dissimulation of our own tensors, our own intense signs within those systems: 'Set dissimulation to work on behalf of intensities. Invulnerable conspiracy, headless, homeless, with neither programme nor project, deploying a thousand cancerous tensors in the bodies of signs' (1993a: 262). This passage, from the last paragraph of *Libidinal Economy*, shows how Lyotard's philosophy avoids ideals independent of the matter at hand, a 'home' or a 'programme'. Instead, it deploys opportunities for desire and for feeling, through tensors, within dispositions.

Conclusion

Lyotard's politics involve variations on two familiar strategies: subversion from within, in the case of the libidinal philosophy; an abstract testimony to difference, in the postmodern condition. However, Lyotard departs from these familiar forms in his assertion that

they are sufficient for a politics, that is, they are justified in themselves and need no further goal or justification. Indeed, to seek any
further goal would be to nullify the acts of testimony and subversion. We should not subvert *for* something or in the aim to achieve a
better state, and neither should we offer testimony in order to right a
wrong or resolve a difference. We cannot know what we release in
terms of future energies and actual possibilities when we subvert a
given state, when we release its intensities. It is satisfaction enough
to know that there has been an intensification or a release of energy.
Similarly, our testimony is not designed to contribute to the emergence of a more harmonious and less unjust state; on the contrary, it
leads to greater and more radical diversity.

Lyotard puts forward models for possible politics. But are those
politics consistent and, ultimately, responsible? In the libidinal
economy, we are committed to acts that undermine systems and
order in favour of a free-floating energy and intensity. But we do not
seek to harness that energy or even seek to control it – quite the
contrary. Is this only destruction and release for their own sakes?
Worse, could the libidinal politics be a wilful opening on to an
unknown and possibly more terrifying and violent future? Lyotard's
answer is that there is a more serious violence of system building
and acting for a predicted future that only his libidinal politics can
avoid and counteract. But this does not refute the claim that his acts
may unwittingly pave the way for greater repression or a state of
violent irrational chaos.

There is a similar problem in the act of testimony for itself. It
leaves us with a feeling for differences, but without the political or
indeed philosophical system to legislate or think through those
differences. Should there be a role for reason after testimony in the
legislation of difference? For Lyotard there cannot be, since reason
and the legislation of difference in a single system cannot recognize
the differends he wishes to testify to. Once again, his philosophy
opens up a field but fails to act or determine acts in such a way as to
guide it into a more just or more peaceful future. Perhaps, then, a
possible role for both his politics is on the margins of another more
systematic and teleological approach, that is, the role of the critic or
of conscience in a speculative politics that recognizes their worth.
But this would be to deny some of their most important tenets
concerning the value and possibility of a just speculative politics.

7
Hegel, Levinas and Capital

Arguments against Hegel

One of the most consistent critical positions to run through Lyotard's work is his opposition to Hegelian philosophy. This critical approach comes out most clearly in *The Differend* and associated essays. There, Hegelian philosophy is presented as the main philosophy denying the differend in general and, hence, particular differends. Instead of absolute differences, in the guise of incommensurable genres or language games, Hegelian philosophy is analysed as putting forward a totalizing metanarrative. That is, in the terms of Lyotard's philosophy of language, Lyotard interprets Hegelian philosophy as offering a genre whose stakes apply to all other genres. This means that differends will not be irresolvable conflicts. The rule of the Hegelian genre is to take the outcome of the conflict as a 'result'. Thereby, a kind of just judgement of the conflict is made simply by recording it. This means that, at least in retrospect, conflicts can be judged justly, in the sense that they contribute to future judgements.

Perhaps the main reason for Lyotard's fear of this genre is the totalizing model it leads to. Each conflict contributes to the genre of the result and it is impossible to claim that a conflict cannot be a result. Lyotard uses the term 'terror' in this context. Terror occurs under totalitarian regimes when subjects cannot make claims to be different or to represent something outside the system. The actual feeling of terror accompanies the realization that it is impossible to make one's claim without at the same time nullifying it. It is impossible to escape from the genre of the result because its rule is to include any claim to fall outside any given rule. Lyotard classes Hegelian philosophy with this technical definition of totalitarianism and terror. He strives to define his philosophy as falling outside Hegelian synthesis, that is, the event must never become a result.

The argument against Hegel takes place mainly in *The Differend* and the essays 'Analysing speculative discourse as a language-game' and 'Discussions, or phrasing "after Auschwitz"' (both in Lyotard 1989b). It involves two related stages: first, a study of Hegel's speculative discourse in the terms of Lyotard's philosophy of language; second, a reference to the Holocaust at Auschwitz as an event beyond the resources of Hegel's philosophy. This latter point is of great importance to Lyotard. Whether a philosophy can bear witness to the Holocaust is its greatest test. He applies this test to his own work – in fact, it could be said to drive his later philosophy. He also uses it against other philosophers, not only Hegel, but also Heidegger: 'I wanted to intervene to try to understand Heidegger's silence on the subject of the *Shoah*, to which Adorno had given the generic name of "Auschwitz"' (Lyotard 1993c: 137).

According to Lyotard, Hegel's speculative philosophy can be understood as a language game whose rule is 'Engender every phrase as the expressed identity of the preceding ones, including the present phrase.' This rule is a challenge to Lyotard's own law of concatenation, because it puts forward an answer to the question of how to link phrases on to one another. Hegel's rule, as stated by Lyotard, appears to solve the problem of the phrase event. It includes all the earlier phrases in the next phrase and thereby does not restrict any of the possible interpretations of the earlier ones. Thus the presentation brought forth by a phrase is left intact by Hegel's rule because it is included in the next phrase. So, in opposition to Lyotard's uncertainty, Hegel puts forward the model of a certainty based on the exhaustive inclusion of all the possibilities of whatever event we have to judge. How can Lyotard counter this rule?

By asking for the basis for the rule. According to Lyotard, either the rule has been conjured out of nothing, or it is a phrase in a concatenation. That is, either the rule is the first phrase – but, then, on what basis is it to be taken as true? Or the rule comes as a phrase in a concatenation – but, then, the phrases preceding it were not concatenated according to the rule. This means that there are concatenations to which the rule was not applied but that the rule must include within its own identity. How can it do this, when there is no way for it to know what phrases preceded it? The only way for those phrases to be known is for them to have been concatenated according to the rule. This cannot be known. Lyotard's questions force the language game of speculative discourse into a difficult position: it must be an arbitrary game based on an arbitrary rule. Therefore the discourse is but one among many, and it cannot claim to disprove Lyotard's law of concatenation. This allows him to conclude: 'But [Hegel's rule] is then merely presupposed and not engendered. If it is not applied from the beginning, there is no necessity in finding it at the end, and if it is not at the end, it wouldn't have been engendered, and it was therefore not the rule that was sought' (Lyotard 1988a: 97).

Lyotard also calls Hegel's rule the rule of the *Resultat* or result. This name explains how the rule works in practice. Take an event involving a contradiction, for example a legal conflict that appears to be beyond resolution: the rule of the result would be able to do as much justice as possible to the conflict by incorporating it within any future judgements. This at least would be a positive result of the conflict: it will have been stored as an experience, a result of the earlier event, something of use to future judgements. Lyotard's case against this practical version of the rule is based on the model of the event of Auschwitz. Following to some extent the lead of the German philosopher Adorno, Lyotard asks: 'What could be the result of Auschwitz?' 'What experience are we to store up for future, more just, reference?' 'How will our taking Auschwitz into account do justice to the victims of that event?' There can be no such result, or experience, or justice. For Lyotard, there can be no experience of Auschwitz because, there, death involved phrases that can never be taken as linking on from one another. The phrases 'Let them die, it's our law' and 'Let us die, it's their law' share no common ground. The first is supposed to put those who hear it in a position of obligation, but they cannot share the law that obliges them to die, a racist law based on the denial of their life. The phrases cannot be included in a later phrase engendered according to Hegel's rule, as an experience for a post-Holocaust community, because the two phrases can never be shared by a community.

Auschwitz can never be resolved into a result: rather, it leads to a silence born of the impossibility of linking on from the two phrases:

> Far indeed from signifying these silences in the phrase of a *Resultat*, 'we' deem it more dangerous to make them speak than to respect them. It is not a concept that results from 'Auschwitz', but a feeling, an impossible phrase, one that would link the S.S. phrase onto the deportee's phrase, or vice-versa. (Lyotard 1988a: 104)

In the event 'Auschwitz', Lyotard rejects a Hegelian result that maintains the void between the two phrases at Auschwitz within a new phrase. Only silences testifying to the void remain: 'Silences, instead of a *Resultat*. These silences interrupt the chain that goes from them, the deported, and from them, the S.S., to we who speak about them' (1988a: 106).

It is important to realize that Lyotard's reference to silence does not imply a politics of silence. This could not make sense in terms of the law of concatenation. According to the law, silence would have the same status as any other phrase unless a silence testified to a differend. Only a sublime silence could function in this way and such a silence could not be the mere absence of commentary. On the contrary, something must occur and yet also exceed its own occurrence. The Hegelian rule, as it is rendered by Lyotard, does not achieve that excess. It fails to testify to the differend, to the original silence. By putting forward a resolution for an event that can never be resolved, the rule attempts the impossible: to put a silence into a cognitive context. The political act must be to testify to silence through creative acts which arouse the feeling of the sublime: something has occurred that cannot simply be understood, or justified, or revenged. In this way, the event remains through testimony. It is not erased through resolutions: '"we" deem it more dangerous to make them speak than to respect them.' Here Lyotard's politics may not have the straightforward appeal of judgements based on specific accounts of reality and on the application of agreed norms. Yet it has an endurance with respect to the event that these judgements can never attain.

Arguments with Levinas

Emmanuel Levinas shares Lyotard's opposition to Hegelian totalization. However, his philosophy presents a further and perhaps closer threat to the philosophy of differends. In fact, the influence of Levinas runs through most of Lyotard's work, at least from *Discours, figure* onwards. The shadow of an ethics of the event haunts his political philosophy of the event. The contrast between a politics and an ethics brings out a potentially serious lack in Lyotard's philosophy. It appears to renounce an ethical stance in politics and action in general. Thus Lyotard seems to be open to accusations of irresponsibility and cynicism, on the one hand, and association with the politics of power – where might is right – on the other. This is why Lyotard's response to Levinas is all-important. There, the ethical void at the heart of his philosophy can either be understood and justified, or highlighted as a fatal flaw.

Where Lyotard develops a fleeting politics around an event beyond representation and understanding, Levinas develops an ethics based on the relation of a self to other persons. This relation is close to the relation of a self to a Lyotard-event, in so far as the other person cannot be known or accurately represented to a self. It is therefore false even to call the other person a person: how could we know? This explains why the other person is in fact referred to, more precisely, as the Other. In Levinas, this relation to the Other leads to an ethics based on an obligation to the Other; put simply, there is an obligation to respect the otherness of others – do not act as if others are the same as yourself. Note here how this ethics defeats the Hegelian law of the result as outlined by Lyotard. It is wrong to apply earlier results to the Other, for this is to assume the Other is the same as us at least to the extent of being able to be treated as a result.

Levinas privileges a certain fixed way of responding to events, that is, an ethical obligation to others as events. Lyotard argues against this privileging of the ethical in order to preserve the fluid, practical and political avant-garde act responding to the event. In effect, he argues that the ethical is only a language game or genre among many: it is equal to all other language games in failing to capture the event. For this reason, it would be wrong for Lyotard's politics to become an ethics; it must maintain its ability to challenge any fixed genre with the creation of new genres. This is not to deny the importance of ethics, or the existence of a properly ethical sphere. Lyotard owes much of his later thinking on ethics to Levinas's and to a meeting of minds on the importance of thinking the ethical moment as an obligation prior to knowledge. Like Lyotard's events, Levinas's Other occurs without the need for knowledge and obliges us to act without telling us how to act: 'Levinas comments on the destituteness of the other: the other arises in my field of perception with the trappings of absolute poverty, without attributes, the other has no place, no time, no essence, the other is nothing but his or her request and my obligation' (Lyotard 1988a: 111).

For Levinas, the face of the other brings forth this obligation because it carries the possibility of expression, what could be said by the other, as my responsibility. The face of the other obliges the self (interiority) to open out on to possibilities that it does not and cannot know: 'The face opens the primordial discourse whose first word is obligation, which no "interiority" permits avoiding' (Levinas 1969: 201). Obligation occurs as the condition for discourse and, therefore, ethics comes prior to knowledge and to politics: 'Pre-existing the disclosure of being in general taken as the basis of knowledge and as meaning of being is the relation with the existent that expresses himself; preexisting the plane of ontology is the ethical plane' (1969: 201). This step from ethical obligation to the claim that ethics comes prior to discourse is the one that is troublesome for Lyotard. In *The Differend* and the important essay 'Levinas' logic' (in Lyotard 1989b), he attempts to draw the fine line between an agreement with Levinas's definition of ethics and his deduction of its primordiality.

Like Lyotard's argument against Hegel, his work on Levinas depends on a translation of his philosophy into Lyotard's philosophy of language. Here, the point will be to distinguish the political philosophy of differends from a Levinasian ethics. Lyotard has to translate an ethical obligation to others into his philosophy of language. The translation is far from straightforward since it demands a move from a philosophy developed in terms of the self and other to the concatenation of phrases. For Levinas, obligation must take the form of an estrangement of the self, or a scandal for the self, in the face of the other. That is, in Levinas's ethics, the self is not truly obliged to the other until an other person is absolutely other. This can only happen when the receiving self is no longer a self, when the self is estranged, made a stranger to itself, or scandalized, profoundly shocked with respect to one's set beliefs and self-identity.

For instance, a stranger turns up at your door asking for protection. So long as that protection is given after a reasoning process or after an appeal to familiar feelings, that act of protection will not satisfy a description of the ethical. This is because the act is based on one's self-knowledge and not on an absolute obligation to the stranger. Knowledge comes after obligation. Ethics has to be described as our obligation to the stranger before we think how to act. So, for Levinas, the appearance of the stranger at the door puts one in a position of obligation before any reference to known values, beliefs, thoughts and so on. In fact, the arrival of the stranger makes one a stranger to one's own beliefs and thought processes and that is why one is obliged to offer protection. How can Lyotard translate this analysis, which depends on a careful description of what occurs to the self in the encounter with the other, to his philosophy of language?

Lyotard translates ethical obligation as a phrase that puts its addressee in the position of being obliged, that is, of being solely the addressee of the phrase and not the addressor of a reaction to the phrase. In obligation the addressee is solely a 'you' as in the phrase 'You must obey'; there is no corresponding phrase of the form 'I must obey', where the self becomes a subject again prior to obeying: 'This is what the I's displacement onto the *you* instance marks: You ought to. Levinas comments upon the destituteness of the other: the other arises in my field of perception with the trappings of absolute poverty' (Lyotard 1988a: 111). This obligation must take place through the feelings of the addressee, for if it took place through thoughts there would be a phrase involving an 'I', 'I think that I must.'

Note how close this comes to Lyotard's understanding of the sublime occurrence of a phrase, where the phrase event is felt but not known. The prescriptive phrase 'You must obey' is therefore ethical when it is taken prior to reflection, that is, prior to a series of cognitive phrases on how to obey. The ethical genre is the set of prescriptive phrases that put us in a position of obligation without explanation and independent of our subsequent actions. Like Levinas's description of the destitution of the self in the face of the other, Lyotard's description of the ethical phrase of obligation allows for the definition of the ethical independent of knowledge and action. In short, the ethical genre and all other genres are incommensurable. For Lyotard and for Levinas, there is ethics only where there is obligation.

So why does Lyotard oppose the primordial aspect of Levinas's ethics? Could we not say that any phrase is ethical in so far as it obliges us to follow on from it (even with our silence)? Why does Lyotard not accept the fundamental ethical dimension of his own philosophy? The answer lies in the incommensurability of the ethical and other genres. Levinas describes the ethical moment in and prior to all others. The obligation that follows from the face of the other is presupposed in discourse and in reason: 'The will is free to assume this responsibility in whatever sense it likes; it is not free to refuse this responsibility itself; it is not free to ignore the meaningful world into which the face of the Other has introduced it' (Levinas 1969: 219).

But for Lyotard this primordial role is not possible. Though there is obligation with a prescriptive phrase, a phrase that follows the phrase of obligation, a phrase of commentary, for example, is not itself obliged. This is equally true for a third person commenting on obligation, Levinas in his own text, or for the 'you' in a phrase of obligation when it becomes an 'I' again in later phrases. Lyotard says the I then becomes 'blind' to the initial obligation. What this means is that obligation does not run through language as a whole. To claim that it does is to give concatenation a stake, that is, to claim that there is a goal which can help us regulate the concatenation of phrases from different regimes. In the case of Levinas, this is the imposition of the stake of the ethical genre: that you shall never be I. So for him, in any concatenation of phrases it is possible to find the obligation or stake of the call to respect the Other. However, for Lyotard, this genre can have no precedence over others; it is but one genre among many and must enter into conflicts, differends, like any other genre.

Why does Lyotard think that the extension of the ethical genre to a legislative function over all others is impossible? Is his law of concatenation a similar extension? He feels close to the event of obligation, but he cannot agree with the priority of an ethical commentary on obligation. On the contrary, there can be no such priority because a phrase of commentary, a cognitive phrase, cannot be ethical since it does not lead to obligation. Unlike Levinas, Lyotard defines obligation as something that can come to pass away:

> A phrase is obligatory if its addressee is obligated. Why he or she is obligated is something he or she can perhaps think to explain. In any case, the explanation requires further phrases . . . Phrases of commentary. The I's blindness may regain the upper hand on the occasion of such phrases. (Lyotard 1988a: 108)

With commentary, or with any concatenation of phrases, the political takes over from the ethical. Lyotard refuses Levinas's extension of ethics because it is possible for a phrase of obligation to be ignored in later phrases. Lyotard chooses a special example of this violence done to obligation in his analysis of the commentary passed on Levinas's own text. It is always possible for commentators to misunderstand or wilfully misinterpret Levinas's work by inscribing it into another genre. In fact, this occurs every time a phrase of commentary follows a phrase of obligation, even when Levinas comments on his own text. The irony is that this wilful misunderstanding in some sense satisfies Levinas's own demand for a respect for the Other, because misunderstanding depends on the obligation not to reduce the Other to the same: 'The irony of the commentator easily goes as far as persecution: the less I understand you, he says to the Levinassian (or divine) text, the more I will obey you by that fact; for, if I want to understand you (in your turn) as a request, then I should not understand you as sense' (Lyotard 1988a: 115).

Thus according to Lyotard there is no primordial role for ethics in discourse or in commentary, instead there is a differend between the ethical genre and the cognitive genre. This differend is shown in the possibility of an ironic and violent misunderstanding of any ethical phrase. The problem for philosophy is not therefore how to uncover the primordial ethical moment in politics, reason or knowledge. It is how to do justice to the incommensurability of knowledge and ethics, but also to all other such conflicts. For this reason Lyotard develops a wider strategy concerned with the testimony to differends, to the irresolvable conflicts that arise out of the incommensurability of all genres: 'Incommensurability, in the sense of the heterogeneity of phrase regimens and of the impossibility of subjecting them to a single law (except by neutralizing them), also marks the relation between either cognitives or prescriptives and interrogatives, per-formatives, exclamatives. . .' (1988a: 128). This does not mean that ethics is unimportant, since we must testify to the differend between ethical obligation and scientific understanding, for example. It does mean, though, that Lyotard cannot accept that obligation and the face of the Other provide us with the basis for a just attitude to differends.

Capitalism and the differend

A further case of Lyotard's critical work against the hegemony of one genre over all others occurs in his critique of capitalism in *The Differend*. The value of this critique is that it shows the political potential of Lyotard's later work in terms of an opposition to the extension of the demand for profitability and economic growth to all domains of life. In simple terms, the language game of capital or the economic genre (in the terminology of *The Differend*) has a stake and a rule for the concatenation of phrases. The rule states that phrases must follow one another according to equal exchanges of time. This exchange of time involves the calculation of the time involved in the production of whatever two phrases exchange between one another – this could be goods, debts, services, promises, favours and so on. The stake imposes an end goal on such concatenations, the goal of gaining time, of efficiency. So the phrase 'Your salary is this much' will be followed by a phrase returning an amount of work (time) equal to the time calculated for the salary.

Lyotard remarks that money is a way of measuring things in terms of time to facilitate the application of the rule. Lyotard's point is: any link can be understood according to this rule, therefore any concatenation can be understood in terms of the goal of the economic genre. Here is a genre that can subject all phrases and genres to its rule and stakes. Lyotard will show how it leads to a hegemony: the dominance of one genre. This dominance can seem to be entirely beneficial to societies; when the increasing wealth, in time or money, is linked to liberal democracies and social emancipation, for example.

So, in contrast to the ambiguous relation to capital in *Libidinal Economy*, in *The Differend* there is an aim to oppose the hegemony of the capitalist economic genre. According to Lyotard, the rule of that genre, to determine the linking of phrases through the exchange of equal amounts of time, and its stake, to save time and hence accumulate money, lead to a dominance of the economic genre over all others. This is because the rule and the stake can be applied with ease to the concatenation of heterogeneous phrase regimens: 'anything at all may be exchanged, on the condition that the time contained by the referent and the time required for the exchange are countable' (Lyotard 1988a: 177). Phrases can become commodities, the point of their links then being to gain time. The phrase 'just in time' applied to production and stock management fits Lyotard's analysis of the stake of the economic genre. The point of the phrase is to show how modern forms of stock management allow time to be gained by eliminating the need for large stocks, so this then increases profitability. Likewise, the practice of 'empowerment' betrays the ability of the economic genre to subject other genres to its rule. The quasi-ethical search for responsibility, autonomy and self-esteem among the lower ranks in firms has been 'satisfied' but according to the stake of gaining time – empowerment improves productivity, it is therefore a good thing.

This hegemony of the economic genre means that it covers up the heterogeneity of phrase regimen and the incommensurability of genres. The economic genre of capital covers up differends, by subjecting any conflict or dispute to the test of profitability. The economic genre asks: which solution to the conflict makes economic sense? The differend does not matter to those who pose that question and this may allow the economic genre to resolve all conflicts, but it does not resolve a differend:

252. The differends between phrase regimen or between genres of discourse are judged to be negligible by the tribunal of capitalism. . . . But if the verdict, always pronounced in favour of gained time, puts an end to

litigations, it may for that very reason aggravate differends. (Lyotard 1988a: 178)

Thus the aim of the philosophy of the differend will be to testify for the differend and against the hegemony of capitalism. In *The Differend*, philosophy set itself up in opposition to the capitalist economic system. This is in stark contrast to *Libidinal Economy* and its advocacy of the dissimulation of tensors within capitalism. Here the difference between the two philosophies is at its greatest. The later philosophy defends a subversive region, the differend, while the earlier philosophy cautions against such illusions and advocates a subversive collaboration.

Thus radically different practical politics come out of related treatments of the event and absolute difference. The realism of libidinal economics is in stark contrast to the pure resistance of the philosophy of the differend. The politics can be attacked on a similar basis; that is, they can be accused of cynicism and lack of effectivity. Yet these attacks must depend on completely different analyses of the faults in Lyotard's philosophy. In the case of the early work, any perceived cynicism comes straight out of a hard-headed attitude towards the relation of society and desire, of intensities and dispositions. It is on the possible mistakes of this study that *Libidinal Economy* is open to criticism. In the case of *The Differend*, the accusation of cynicism is a secondary factor. The problem lies in the distance imposed on politics by the rejection of any possibility of just resolutions. Instead, we are asked to pursue a politics of irresolution, of the testimony to the differend. Here the lack of effective action is the problem. It is not that Lyotard is accused of lacking in the will to be just; it is rather that he is insisting on too high a criterion for justice. Any attack on this approach will concentrate on the source of this extremism and distanciation: the analysis of the feeling of the sublime. In both cases, though, it would be a mistake to accuse Lyotard of lacking a committed politics or an ethically acceptable theoretical basis for action.

8

Critical debates

Lyotard, Deleuze and Guattari

Lyotard's work has given rise to a number of intense arguments. The majority of these follow on from his description of the post-modern condition. The work on the libidinal economy gave offence to many French Marxists (including his old colleagues from *Socialisme ou Barbarie* – *Libidinal Economy* contains a vitriolic attack on Cornelius Castoriadis, one of the main figures in *Socialisme ou Barbarie*, see Lyotard 1993a: 116–20), but it did not lead to many sustained critical reactions. Perhaps the only exceptions to this trend are works by Gilles Deleuze and Félix Guattari, which run very close to *Libidinal Economy*, in particular to its descriptions of the Freudian libidinal economy, structuralism and Marxist theory. In fact, 'Capitalisme énergumène', one of Lyotard's best studies of capitalism in the libidinal economic period (included in *Des Dispositifs pulsionnels*), is a study and criticism of Deleuze and Guattari's treatment of capitalism in *Anti-Oedipus*: 'There must be an evacuation of the nostalgic mode of speaking and seeing: it must escape through the hole Deleuze and Guattari punch in Western discourse' (Lyotard 1980a: 33). In many ways, Lyotard's work on Deleuze and Guattari can be seen as prefiguring their work on capitalism in *A Thousand Plateaus*. No doubt the difficult style of *Libidinal Economy*, its vicious attacks on 'past friends' and its libidinal tone and examples contributed to the lack of attention given to it over the years. This lack of comment is certainly a missed opportunity, given the book's rich and provoking description of contemporary society in terms of libidinal systems. *Libidinal Economy* is due a reverse in fortunes.

Perhaps this reversal will come from the association of Gilles Deleuze and Félix Guattari's libidinal materialism, as put forward in *Anti-Oedipus* and *A Thousand Plateaus*, with Lyotard's libidinal economics. However, despite the parallels between the two bodies of work, an explicit critique of Lyotard's early work is made by Deleuze and Guattari. The criticism turns on the point that in the libidinal philosophy, from *Discours, figure* to (at least) *Libidinal Economy*, the concept of intensity is developed in terms of limit events, that is, in terms of a paradoxical passing of energy from beyond a limit defined as an event. This implies that the philosophy of libidinal economics posits a beyond as the ungraspable source of energy and new forms, a zone which is infinitely valuable and yet unknown. For Deleuze and Guattari, this conception of the event and the limit introduces a negative dualism into Lyotard's materialism. Instead of putting forward a philosophy of immanence, where all events are immanent to a world consisting of different but connected planes, Lyotard is accused of constructing another philosophy of transcendence. His philosophy is seen as replicating the religious dependence on the theatrical set-up, where the scene refers to another more real but lost world and where the source of all truth and value is transcendent to the world in which the play develops.

Deleuze and Guattari make this point in terms of a reintroduction of castration and the idea of the Other into Lyotard's libidinal philosophy:

> Any effort to determine the non-human nature of sex, for example the 'Great Other', whilst conserving the myth of castration, is doomed. What does Lyotard mean, in his otherwise so deep commentary on Marx's text, when he assigns the opening of the non-human as having to be 'the entry of the subject into desire through castration'? Long live castration so that desire be strong? We only desire well when we desire phantasms? What a perverse idea, human, all too human. An idea that comes from bad faith, and not from the unconscious. Anthropomorphic molar representation reaches its zenith in that which it grounds, the ideology of lack. (Deleuze and Guattari 1977: 351)

In this passage, Deleuze and Guattari are referring to the section 'Sexe non-humain' in *Discours, figure* (Lyotard 1971: 138–41) where Lyotard applies his interpretation of desire in Freud. There sexual desire is defined not as a desire for the other sex and hence a reuniting of the sexes, but a desire for a non-human sex. Therefore desire is for an exteriority, the death of the human. The full sentence from *Discours, figure* contrasts an event which can be reinscribed into a full representation with an event, desire, which is a violent disturbance of any effort to represent:

> When, provided with the North pole, we discover the South pole, we are not grasped by an irreparable event, which requires all the strength of the imagination to be filled with representations and requires the misleading of the affect in order to be displaced on to other representatives. It is rather to the contrary, such a discovery is a complement, it is a recognition. But the entry of the subject into desire through castration is always something like its death. The No of the non-human sex, inhuman (*unmenschlich*), indicates difference, another position (scene) which deposes the scene of consciousness, the scene of discourse and the scene of reality. (1971: 141)

Lyotard's use of the Freudian death drive, found in *Libidinal Economy*, was already the basis for his study of desire in the earlier work:

> in imagining the real difference to be between the human sex and the non-human sex, Marx comes very close to that which will become Freud's object of research, since he refuses to cicatrize the difference of the sexes into the masculine/feminine opposition, since he imagines, if only for a second, in the fact of human sex (masculine and feminine) an irremissible violence, the reference to an exteriority, the non-human sex. (1971: 141)

But in *Discours, figure* desire is defined explicitly in terms of the death drive *and* castration, a term which introduces a radical negation into desire. For Deleuze and Guattari, this cannot fail to plunge Lyotard's libidinal philosophy back into religiosity and away from the affirmative philosophy that he defends in his early work. This is because desire and intensity cannot fail to be treated in terms of the negation of castration, and hence in terms of the irremediable lack so despised by Lyotard in libidinal economy. If we follow Deleuze and Guattari's remark, the philosophy of the event, as it becomes developed in terms of the figure or the tensor (in *Libidinal Economy*), reproduces the 'all too human' negative definition of desire in terms of the absolute limit of the event.

This criticism is all the more powerful since it turns Lyotard's critique of theatricality and religiosity (the setting up of a scene turned towards a transcendent plane that it can never reach, but whence it derives truth and power) against his own philosophy. However, although it cannot be denied that Lyotard's libidinal economy is developed on an explicit use of castration in desire, and on an implicit dependence on the ideas of lack and negation in his philosophy of the event, this does not necessarily imply that his philosophy depends on a transcendent plane or is a form of religiosity. This is because Lyotard's conception of the event refuses to account for, or value, the set-ups which channel intensity in terms of some or other transcendent alluded to through a set-up or scene privileged over all others. On the contrary, the event of intensity, as developed through the tensor or the figure, specifically disallows any such move: the event is an absolute limit and there is no place for a narrative on the beyond from within any given set-up or disposition.

Thus Lyotard's aim of becoming a good conductor of intensity never specifies the best way to conduct; rather, in the concept of dissimulation, he advocates exploiting given set-ups by releasing the intensity stored in their tensors. This involves destroying their claims to a privileged access to truth and undermining their 'religious' hold on the event. This is made clear in *Discours, figure* where Lyotard ascribes the death of the subject, along with the destruction of the 'scenes' of consciousness, discourse and reality, to the event of desire. When Lyotard writes of a scene other than that of human consciousness, in 'Sexe non-humain', he is not referring to another world 'off-stage'; rather, he is underlining the status of this world as a necessary proliferation of incompossible worlds.

Yet it is difficult not to agree with Deleuze and Guattari that the condition for incompossibility, the event of intensity, depends on a radical negation, that is, upon its status as a radical limit. Lyotard's philosophy, it would appear, is bound to reproduce the very set-up it seeks hardest to escape. This is the price of Lyotard's search for an absolute refutation of the claims to absolute truth of any given set-up, disposition or narrative. However, it is only thanks to the common ground shared by Lyotard's libidinal economics and Deleuze and Guattari's libidinal materialism that this point can be made. It is only because there is a shared sensibility to the destructive power of negation that an argument can develop on the point of whether a philosophy of the event as limit can escape the trap of setting up a plane of transcendence and hence of developing a new set of illegitimate values and truths based on that plane.

If Deleuze and Guattari's criticisms are updated to include Lyotard's work in *The Differend*, then they take on even greater force. The philosophy of the sublime does appear to depend on a form of castration. The contradictory feelings of pleasure and pain, or terror and delight, forbid any communication beyond a testimony to a limit event. Yet this barrier marks the presence of a hallowed realm:

the source of absolute difference and of the events that force us to bear testimony to that which cannot be understood. Here it is difficult to escape the accusation of religiosity. The sublime belongs to an important religious tradition. Indeed, Barnett Newman's art – possibly Lyotard's most important practical example of the sublime – lends itself to religious interpretations and contexts (Newman's designs for synagogues and many of his famous 'zip' paintings are explicitly religious). Lyotard does attempt to separate his work from the religious sublime. For example, his use of the term 'the jews' in *Heidegger et 'les juifs'* is carefully developed in secular terms. Despite these efforts, it is difficult to detect a great distance between the religious and the secular sublime when the issue is 'the opening of the non-human' as 'the entry of the subject into desire through castration'.

Further indications of this split between Lyotard and Deleuze and Guattari can be found in Lyotard's interpretations of Deleuze and Guattari's work. Where they struggle to avoid set-ups which depend on limits and castration, Lyotard assigns metaphors to their texts which cannot help reminding us of transcendence instead of the immanence sought by Deleuze and Guattari. Thus, in 'Capitalisme énergumène', he describes *Anti-Oedipus* as a 'pantograph', a disposition that carries energy from one source to another, that is, a miraculous and productive bridging of a gap. Even in describing a text violently opposed to castration, Lyotard cannot avoid the image of an abyss and a sublime fragile passageway. The early nineteenth-century picturesque sublime and the paintings of impossible Alpine bridges on the verge of destruction could serve as a precedent here. Later, in a work dedicated to Deleuze ('Ligne générale', in *Moralités postmodernes*), Lyotard speaks of an 'inhuman region' to be preserved from the human region of rights. This region is made present to us through the testimony of silence: 'That silence is an exception to the reciprocity of rights; but it is also its legitimation. We should recognize the absolute right of this "second existence", given that it gives right to rights. But, since it escapes rights, it can only ever be satisfied with an amnesty' (1993b: 10).

This characterization of and offering to Gilles Deleuze shows the gap between a philosophy of immanence and a philosophy dependent on a return to transcendence. Deleuze insists on *one* plane, in order to defeat the castration of desire in the essential set-up of religion. Lyotard, on the other hand, depends on two realms that can never be reconciled and whose separation is the source of justice, 'it gives rights to rights.'

Thus, in contrast to critics who accuse Lyotard's politics of cynicism and lack of ethics, Deleuze and Guattari allow for a reading of Lyotard as still too ethical and religious – still too steeped in the negative and deluded desire for the Good independent of the matter of desire. To be positioned in this way, between a rational politics for the Good and a radical libidinal materialism, adds interest to Lyotard's work. His philosophy allows for a meeting of these opposed camps. Through different criticisms of Lyotard, it becomes possible to articulate a wide scene of contemporary philosophy and politics.

Critical approaches to *The Postmodern Condition*

The Postmodern Condition, unlike *Libidinal Economy*, has led to a profusion of responses covering the whole spectrum of philosophical and political opinion. This reaction to a single book is somewhat unfortunate because it has tended to eclipse Lyotard's better work on similar topics, in *The Differend*. For an example of readings of Lyotard that take *The Postmodern Condition* on too simple a level, see Richard Rorty, 'Le Cosmopolitanisme sans émancipation: en réponse à Jean-François Lyotard' (1985), which includes a discussion between Lyotard and Rorty, and Rorty, 'Habermas and Lyotard on postmodernity'(1991). There are, however, some critical approaches that take the full description of the postmodern condition into consideration, and those are the ones that are of interest here.

Two forms of response stand out. Broadly, these are:

1 The response from thinkers who remain in the modern tradition. They are politically left-wing and are critical of what they perceive to be reactionary aspects of Lyotard's work. Their formal critique of Lyotard's philosophy turns on the possibility of well-founded just judgements, as opposed to his description of a plurality of conflicting language games and a form of fleeting politics based on the feeling of the sublime.

2 The response from other thinkers in the poststructuralist school, whose works come close to his in terms of the opposition to the hegemony of metanarratives. These thinkers tend to shy away from Lyotard's politics, based on recognizable conflicts, and to advocate moves towards an ethical respect of difference in general or a philosophical commitment to the possibility of difference.

The first category includes Seyla Benhabib's 'Epistemologies of postmodernism: a rejoinder to Jean-François Lyotard'(1984), Jacques Bouveresse's *Rationalité et cynisme* (1984), Peter Dews's *Logics of Disintegration* (1987), Luc Ferry and Alain Renaut's *La Pensée 68* (1985), Manfred Frank's *Was ist Neostrukturalismus?* (1984) and Gérard Raulet's 'From modernity as a one-way street to postmodernity as dead-end' (1984). The second category includes works by Geoff Bennington (1988) and Jacques Derrida (1992), Philippe Lacoue-Labarthe's 'Où en étions-nous?' (1985) and essays by Jean-Luc Nancy (1985, 1991).

It should be noted that by far the most incisive readings of Lyotard are those by Geoff Bennington and Jean-Luc Nancy. The essence of Nancy's argument in 'Dies irae' and 'Lapsus judicii' is that Lyotard's opposition of the differend and a differend cannot be maintained. That is, if there is a general differend between the presentation brought forth by any phrase and any situation of that presentation, then to speak of a particular differend is already to fail to do justice to the differend in general. This is because the isolation of a particular conflict is already a situation of a presentation. See also David Ingram's perceptive use of Nancy's arguments in 'The postmodern Kantianism of Arendt and Lyotard' (1992). Jacques Derrida's 'Before the law' (1992) does not appear to be concerned with Lyotard, but it was given, originally, at a colloquium on Lyotard's work and on politics. The key to an understanding of the critical value of the text is an understanding of categories. In 'Before the law', Derrida offers a deconstruction of the notion of well-defined legal categories. The damage such a deconstruction can inflict on Lyotard's differend is very great because the differend is a conflict between well-defined language games. Here, the definition in question is the incommensurability of specific language games or genres. See also the remarks by Derrida and Lyotard's response after 'Discussions, or phrasing "after Auschwitz"' in *The Lyotard Reader* (Lyotard 1989b: 386–9).

In addition to the categories given above, there are some rogue critical positions tending to concentrate on one area of Lyotard's work. This is particularly true of his work on the sublime and avant-garde art (an example of this kind of criticism can be found in the work of Paul Crowther: 'If, therefore, we are to have a theoretically adequate notion of the sublime, we must – in a way Lyotard does not – show some *logical* kinship between its negative and positive components' (1992: 201).

Finally, there are thinkers who share many of Lyotard's conclusions and seek to push his ideas further, or to apply them to new areas and challenges. Andrew Benjamin's work on philosophy and translation fits this category, in particular where Benjamin develops his study of 'anoriginal heterogeneity', a description of matter that comes very close to Lyotard's description of the phrase event: 'Difference understood as original difference – differential plurality as anoriginal – both emerges in, as well as provides the conditions of possibility for conflicts of interpretation' (Benjamin 1989: 38); see also his *The Plural Event* (1993). The same can also be said of Geoff Bennington's *Lyotard: Writing the Event* (1988), where Bennington draws Lyotard's work into the sphere of deconstruction through an intricate weave of commentary and Lyotard's texts.

The point of the conclusion here, though, will not be to select all of these categories of critique for further examination. Instead, two model critiques will be put forward, in order to bring attention to two possible critical approaches to Lyotard's work. The first critique is developed by Manfred Frank, following Jürgen Habermas. The second critique follows points made by Jacques Derrida and Jean-Luc Nancy; my intent, in this case, will be to draw out Lyotard's defence against the claim that any categories or dispositions treated by Lyotard must be arbitrary.

Manfred Frank on Habermas and Lyotard

Though a specific debate between Jean-François Lyotard and Jürgen Habermas never took place, a number of commentators have sought to invent one or at least to trace its main arguments (see Rorty 1991; Steuerman 1992; Benhabib 1984). Indeed, virtually all of Lyotard's most severe critics develop their analyses through an unfavourable comparison of his and Habermas's positions. This contrast stands out because it has the merit of bringing together theoretical, political and ethical criticisms. It is therefore all-important in any assessment of Lyotard's philosophy. It is also a key moment in the debate that has come to oppose modernist and postmodernist thinkers.

By far the best creation of a precise debate between the two thinkers is by Manfred Frank. A version of the debate exists in German, *Die Grenzen der Verständigung. Ein Geistergespräch zwischen Lyotard und Habermas* (1988b). There is also a version (1988a) published in a French collection on Lyotard's work, 'Dissension et consensus selon Jean-François Lyotard et Jürgen Habermas' in *Jean-François Lyotard: réécrire la modernité*, a special issue of *Les Cahiers de Philosophie*; this collection is of particular interest since it includes an answer to Manfred Frank by Jacob Rogozinski, 'Argumenter avec Manfred Frank?', and related accounts of Lyotard's work and the postmodern by Albrecht Wellmer and Dick Veerman. Frank's argument brings together critical points of varying theoretical complexity. Most can be traced back to a key accusation: Lyotard falls prey to a performative contradiction. His argument is self-defeating because it depends on a form of shared rationality that it wishes to deny. However, each point made by Frank has its own force and specific criticism; they are as follows:

1 Lyotard cannot make a moral commitment to the victims of a differend and, in particular, to the victims of Nazi gas chambers.
2 In *The Differend*, propositions can only be verified and taken to be correct if a *counterfactual* intersubjective plane is presupposed.
3 According to Lyotard, the heterogeneity of phrase regimen depends on rules that belong to clearly defined genres. There is no justification for this supposition.
4 Lyotard's argument is viciously circular. He claims that statements on the differend can have no universal validity. However, this claim must include the statement on the invalidity of statements.
5 A linguistic system that has the potential to be shared is the condition for the differend. It is also therefore the basis for its resolution.
6 Lyotard's critique of the subject renders pointless any testimony to the differend, since there would be no one to testify for.
7 To elevate the silence that follows the assassination of a subject to the level of a valid norm (Lyotard's law of concatenation) is cynical and contradictory. One should testify to the disappearance and not welcome it. Any testimony presupposes the discourse of subjectivity and intersubjectivity.

The first point draws our attention to the problems inherent in Lyotard's politics of testimony. He aims to testify to irresolvable conflicts, differends, that are indicated to us through sublime feelings. It is incumbent on us then to create ways of communicating this conflict to others, notably through the techniques of the avant-garde in art and literature. However, as Lyotard notes, in the case of the victims of the gas chamber we have gone beyond an irresolvable conflict: one side has eradicated the other. So, following Manfred Frank, there is no differend to testify to in Lyotard's sense of an irreconcilable difference. Rather, there is a crime that must be righted as best we can and this demands positive forms of action such as the recovery of historical records. But this point about the victims of the gas chambers is also the basis for a general criticism of the philosophy of differend and the politics of testimony. What is the point of testifying to a difference in this case, and indeed in any differend, if we cannot take a positive stand on behalf of those who suffer and have suffered? Testimony is only the first step in 'moral commitment'; the next must be to alleviate the suffering and do it justice. This conception of moral commitment is incompatible with Lyotard's position since he denies that we can justly do anything further than testify. Then why testify at all? In particular, why testify to crimes where the victim has been eradicated?

Frank pursues the criticism by showing what Lyotard's philosophy omits or lacks and yet presupposes: an intersubjective plane characterized by a shared linguistic system. Frank's second point seeks a basis for the validity of Lyotard's claims. How can Lyotard argue for the differend without expecting his audience to understand his arguments and share his feelings and aims? Does this shared understanding not provide the basis for an 'intersubjective plane', a common way of communicating and testing the validity of arguments? Frank's seventh point defines this criticism in terms of a shared linguistic system. That is, Lyotard's arguments on the differend presuppose a common system, one that allows us to understand him; but, if this is the case, then this common system contradicts his basis definition of the differend as an irresolvable difference, since the shared linguistic system provides us with a minimal basis for the resolution of conflicts. This is why the Habermasian criticism concerning Lyotard's performative contradiction is difficult to refute, since Lyotard's efforts to prove the universal validity of his theory point towards a means for resolving his claims about the differend and the event.

The difficulty is made clear in Frank's fourth point. Lyotard's philosophy of language involves the paradox of a universal claim against the possibility of universal claims. In the law of concatenation, he asserts that we must follow one phrase with another, but that we cannot know how to follow any given phrase. Yet if we apply the assertion to itself, we are presented with a paradox since, at least in this case, we know that we must follow one phrase with another and that we cannot know how. If we deny that minimal knowledge on

Lyotard's assertion then his whole system collapses. The 'vicious circularity' of his theory is brought out here. It appears that Lyotard cannot ground his philosophy without having to appeal to paradoxical statements such as the law of concatenation.

The final points made by Frank attempt to go beyond the paradoxical and circular nature of Lyotard's argument by showing that the only consistent act of testimony is one that supposes that we can recognize those whom we testify for as subjects, that is, people with whom we share the use of a common linguistic system. In turn, this shows the negative and damaging aspect of Lyotard's testimony to differends. It leaves those who have suffered a wrong in silence. In fact, it puts forward testimony to the necessity of that silence as the end or final goal of a politics. But this is 'cynical and contradictory' because that testimony presupposes a way out of silence through the intersubjective plane of language. In effect, according to Frank and other Habermasians, Lyotard's events and differends are not ends in themselves, barriers to any effective political acts of mediation and reconciliation: they must be the basis for rational discourse on difference according to a shared intersubjective linguistic system.

It can be argued that these critical points depend on not following Lyotard's argument into his discussion of the feeling of the sublime and the politics of the avant-garde. This is made clear in Frank's third point, the 'justification' he seeks (and does not find) for the heterogeneity of phrase regimen lies in the work on the sublime as it applies to the analysis of genres. Similarly, in terms of his first critical point, there is the possibility of political and philosophical action in the sublime testimony to the differend. It is true that this would not be called ethical, since ethical obligation is a genre among many (see Lyotard's critique of Levinas). Yet it is recognizably moral in the sense that it is a non-selfish and just action. Lyotard's philosophy is not a quietism, though it does challenge established moral positions through a rethinking of the just. This response also addresses Frank's seventh point on the cynicism of Lyotard's law of concatenation. Lyotard never supports a forgetting of the Holocaust. From his earliest work he has born testimony to Auschwitz, as he does again in *The Differend*.

It is the question of how to testify that concerns Lyotard. His philosophy of the sublime is precisely an answer to the question. In his somewhat acerbic article on Frank's criticisms, Jacob Rogozinski (1988) makes exactly this point. In fact, he expresses his outrage at Frank's misreading of Lyotard. This is unfair since Frank puts forward a careful reading of Lyotard and since the argument between Lyotard and Frank brings together two thoughtful, though radically opposed, positions. However, Rogozinski is right in observing that Lyotard attacks 'universal procedures of validation' but does not follow this by concluding that we cannot testify to Auschwitz. To support his argument, Rogozinski draws Frank's attention to the following passage from *The Differend*: 'But then, the historian must break with the monopoly over history granted to the cognitive regimen of phrases, and he or she must venture forth by lending his or her ear to what is not presentable under the rules of knowledge' (Lyotard 1988a: 57). It is entirely possible to be cynical about the cognitive regimen of phrases without affirming a quietist attitude to what Lyotard testifies to each time he returns to the name Auschwitz.

Rogozinski then goes on to identify the key difference between Frank and Lyotard. It is this difference that allows Frank to make his second point on the presupposition of an intersubjective plane, his fourth point on the logical circularity of Lyotard's argument and his fifth point on the presupposition of a shared linguistic system. According to Rogozinski, Lyotard attempts to think outside the boundaries of the argumentative genre, dependent on 'the logically coherent concatenation of cognitive phrases regulated by determinant judgement'. Frank, on the other hand 'refuses' to break with the monopoly of that genre. This is why he reads a logical contradiction into each of Lyotard's essays at 'writing the event' (to use Bennington's felicitous expression). It is also why this genre is seen to be the condition for any valid philosophical argument. However, this reading depends on a prior acceptance of the dominance of the argumentative genre and its logical rules. Yet Lyotard's point has always been that this genre cannot do justice to events. Indeed, this is why Lyotard's writing often takes the form of avant-garde essays that eschew a simple presentation of an argument, in favour of a style better suited to the opening up of a space for feelings and events; in Rogozinski's words: '[Frank] builds the argumentative genre into a meta-genre to which all other phrase regimens must be subordinated, including the quasi-phrases of feelings or affects' (1988: 191). The question here will always be whether Lyotard is right to dismiss the genre that Frank judges to be the condition for any concatenation of phrases. The key is in the topic of feelings and affects: can we account for them from within the argumentative genre? Or is Lyotard's philosophy of the event a better way of doing justice to them?

Lyotard and deconstruction

A model for a deconstruction of Lyotard's philosophy, unlike the criticism based on the transcendental subject, will not appeal to a basis outside that philosophy. Instead, its point will be to play aspects of Lyotard's philosophy off against each other. This does not imply that the deconstruction will lack political goals; rather, it implies that in order to achieve these goals it refuses to ground a philosophy on a positive, external basis. Any political or ethical points will be made through the specific deconstruction, rather than through an abstract theoretical criticism of Lyotard's philosophy dependent on the edification of an alternative position. A serious outcome of this remark is the problematization of the résumé of deconstruction given by me. Indeed, if deconstruction concentrates on practical work within a corpus of texts and if the success of deconstruction depends on individual performances on the body of Lyotard's work, the work in hand can only take on the status of caricature. For this reason, there is also a discussion here of Derrida's 'Before the law'. It is also worthwhile to look further and refer to Jean-Luc Nancy on Lyotard (see above) or to Geoff Bennington's complex, but ultimately rewarding, *Lyotard: Writing the Event*.

From the point of view of a sketch of deconstruction, the most interesting aspects to set to work against each other in Lyotard's philosophy are in *The Differend*; in particular, where he works with the differend in general and particular differends. There a deconstruction can seek to highlight the uneasy relation between the general term and particular differends. The projected outcome of this move will be to undermine Lyotard's distinction between the differend in general and particular differends. In turn, this subversion will problematize Lyotard's work on specific differends, by showing how they too can be divided into ever more complex distinctions. It can also highlight his reliance on the quasi-transcendental definition of the differend in general. In the philosophy of language from *The Differend*, this move equates to a double strategy of a practical attack on the privileging of specific language games and on the elevation of the feeling of the sublime to the status of a universal principle in the law of concatenation. Thus the act of testifying to the differend in general will be put in the context of the act testifying to an ever-increasing number of relative distinctions and conflicts, that is, incommensurability will have to give way to an endless demultiplication of differences.

How would such a deconstruction work? Firstly, it would draw attention to the inconsistencies in Lyotard's deductions of specific differends (to the artificial nature of the limits he imposes on language games and genres or to the inaccurate definition he must impose on specific cases within those genres). Secondly, it would trace back Lyotard's statements on incommensurability to the feeling of the sublime as itself an ill-defined and problematic category. In general, the deconstructions would follow the following abstract arguments *but in practical performances*. If the law of concatenation holds true, then there is no absolutely just way of linking on from any given phrase. This remark applies to any possible link and therefore it applies to the act that testifies to a particular differend. There can be no legitimate act of testimony, as a link on from a particular phrase involved in a particular differend, because there is no legitimate way of singling out that particular differend. According to the law of concatenation, there is nothing to separate an act of testimony and an act that perpetrates a differend. Thus the only truly just link is one that bears testimony to the law of concatenation, that is, an act that bears testimony to the differend in general. Yet the differend in general is itself based on a specific and ill-defined feeling. Lyotard's definition of the feeling of the sublime allows for a blurring of the distinctions between different feelings, pleasure and pain, and a dissociation of its association with specific sublime occurrences, in favour of association with the beautiful, or even with the decorative and the picturesque. In practical terms, this could become an injunction not to single out particular differends but to insist on an ever more complex network of ungrounded differences and conflicts.

These potential deconstructive moves would not necessarily pull Lyotard away from a philosophy of positive political moves, but they would thwart his efforts to define victims of differends as victims of irresolvable conflicts. In his defence, a set of counter-moves would have to be set in motion to preserve the all-important general side of his philosophy. In the case of this outline of a deconstruction, the avant-garde act associated with the feeling of the sublime could be defended as a testimony to the differend in general while, through its status as a transient act, it could be defended as admitting to further moves that cancel out the initial differends. This is the strength of a fleeting politics; it allows positive political moves while avoiding the trap of certainty.

Yet how close is this politics of flight to the politics of deferral and deconstruction put forward in Derrida's 'Before the law'? Derrida's study of literature and law, through an intricate and open-ended consideration of Kafka's 'Before the law' and *The Trial*, can be seen as adding to and refining Lyotard's work on the law of concatenation in its relation to incommensurable genres (in this case the genre of literature). Derrida's demultiplication of remarks on the law and Kafka's text allows for a productive link with Lyotard's work on differends, but this richness also presents challenges to Lyotard's dependence on the law and on heterogeneous categories: 'This has hardly been a categorical reading. I have ventured glosses, multiplied interpretations, asked and diverted questions, abandoned decipherings in mid-course, left enigmas intact; I have accused, defended, praised, subpoenaed' (Derrida 1992: 217). In particular, Derrida develops an interpretation of law as event which comes close to Lyotard's understanding of the event as accompanied by a law (the law of concatenation):

> At the moment when the man comes to his end without reaching his end. The entrance is destined for and awaits him alone; he arrives there but cannot arrive at arriving. Thus runs the account of the event which arrives at not arriving, which manages not to happen. (1992: 210)

Indeed, Derrida's account of the man standing before the law as 'the event which arrives at not arriving' appears to encapsulate Lyotard's account of the event as a presentation that must always elude any situation, as necessarily beyond any final representation or description. Further, Derrida brings this description of the law as event to bear on the presentation brought forth with the literary text:

> We are *before* this text that, saying nothing definite and presenting no identifiable content before the story itself, except for an endless *différance*, till death, nonetheless remains strictly intangible. Intangible: by this I understand inaccessible to contact, impregnable, and ultimately ungraspable, incomprehensible – but also that which we have not the *right* to touch. (1992: 211)

Again, Lyotard's conception of the event as a sublime limit for thought finds echoes in Derrida's description of the literary text as marking a passage into the unidentifiable and intangible. This parallel is developed further when he writes of not having the right to touch (or think) beyond this limit, in the same way as Lyotard posits the differend on a law. There is incommensurability because there are events and the event of law as text (Derrida) and as phrase (Lyotard).

Thus for Derrida the category of literature arrives with the events, the texts, of literature and yet remains beyond any given law or definition:

> In this sense, Kafka's text tells us perhaps of the being-before the law of any text. It does so by ellipsis, at once advancing and retracting it. It belongs not only to the literature of a given period, inasmuch as it is itself before the law (which it articulates), before a certain type of law. The text also points obliquely to literature, speaking of itself as literary effect – and thereby exceeding the literature of which it speaks. (Derrida 1992: 215)

So the category arrives with the event in the same way as a differend between categories, in so far as the text announces a new literature that exceeds literature in the same way as the feeling of the sublime defines genres as incommensurable or gives a feeling of the law of concatenation as a limit. Like Lyotard's event, associated with the feeling of the sublime, Derrida's text is at the same time an advance and a retreat, an event that invites and forbids passage, or says 'You must follow, but there is no right way to follow.' Again, Derrida captures the spirit of Lyotard's later work when he describes Kafka's text – and by extension any literary text – as that which exceeds 'the literature of which it speaks'. The category of literature can only be defined 'obliquely', in a way which accords with the events of literature, literary texts.

However, where Lyotard exploits the double aspect of the law of concatenation and the feeling of the sublime to testify to differends and to the incommensurability of genres, Derrida extends his deconstruction to the differend and to genres or categories. This is because, in Derrida's deconstruction, the condition for excess is not a specific feeling and the awareness of specific absolute limits, but the possibility of endless deferrals and disseminations. This possibility is an endless *différance* and not the barrier of an absolute difference. Where Lyotard sets up an event marking an arrival or passage through a limit that can never be crossed again, Derrida marks a line that can always be crossed and never fixed. But, therefore, Derrida marks a line that can never be crossed once and for all, and therefore he also marks a limit that is always fixed, a limit for final crossings. The effects are similar, because both philosophers undermine the speculative crossing of the limit by testifying for the limit brought forth by an event. However, Derrida's *différance* also defers and disseminates Lyotard's incommensurable genres and feeling of the sublime, for they too can be crossed and this is why they are limits:

In the fleeting moment when it plays the law, a literature passes literature. It is on both sides of the line that separates law from the outlaw, it
splits the being-before-the-law, it is at once, like the man from the coun-
try, 'before the law' and 'prior to the law' ['"devant la loi" et "avant la
loi"']. (Derrida 1992: 216)

Can Lyotard's philosophy accommodate this passing of the line
'that separates the law and the outlaw' or does Derrida's study of
literature initiate a fatal deconstruction of the limits which ground
Lyotard's philosophy of differends? No doubt, if this change is to
occur, differends will be 'passed' and will depend on being 'passed'.
Their political status will change, they will no longer be absolute
differences to be testified to, but differences to be passed *but never
finally*. A positive definition and feeling will have been lost in this
accommodation, but perhaps the critical force of Lyotard's philosophy, in so far as it opposes totalization and the possibility of absolute knowledge, will remain secure.

Yet is it possible to think of Lyotard's political acts as deconstructions and not as the erection of absolute limits? Is it possible to
think of a philosophy of differends without the feeling of the sublime? Is it possible to cut a philosophy off from the condition of its
law and yet still retain its force? The following passage from 'Before
the law' sets out the stakes of these questions:

We touch here on one of the most difficult points of this whole problematic: when we must recover language without language, language beyond language, this interplay of forces which are mute but already haunted
by writing, where the conditions of a performative are established, as are
the rules of the game and the limits of subversion. (Derrida 1992: 216)

Lyotard's interplay of forces in the feeling of the sublime allows for
this 'recovery of language without language', the event of language,
but it does not allow for the haunting of the beyond by language, for
that would be to destroy the limit on which his philosophy depends.

References

Quotations from French language sources below are my own translation.

Aristotle 1925: *Nicomachean Ethics*, trans. W. D. Ross. Oxford: Oxford University Press.
Baudrillard, Jean 1972: *For a Critique of the Political Economy of the Sign*, trans. C. Levin. St Louis: Telos.
—— 1975: *The Mirror of Production*, trans. M. Poster. St Louis: Telos.
Benhabib, Seyla 1984: Epistemologies of postmodernism: a rejoinder to Jean-François Lyotard. *New German Critique*, 33, Fall, 103–26.
Benjamin, Andrew 1989: *Translation and the Nature of Philosophy*. London: Routledge.
—— 1993: *The Plural Event*. London: Routledge.
Bennington, Geoffrey 1988: *Lyotard: Writing the Event*. Manchester: Manchester University Press.
Bouveresse, Jacques 1984: *Rationalité et cynisme*. Paris: Minuit.
Burke, Edmund 1757 (1958): *Philosophical Inquiry into the Origin of our Ideas of the Sublime and the Beautiful*. London: Routledge.
Burns, Robert 1990: To a mouse. In W. Wallace (ed.), *Poetical Works of Robert Burns*, Edinburgh: Chambers.
Carroll, David 1987: *Paraesthetics: Foucault, Lyotard, Derrida*. London: Routledge.
Crowther, Paul 1992: Les Immmatériaux and the postmodern sublime. In A. Benjamin (ed.), *Judging Lyotard*, London: Routledge.
Deleuze, Gilles and Guattari, Félix 1977: *Anti-Oedipus: Capitalism and Schizophrenia*, trans. R. Hurley, M. Seem and H. Lane. New York: Viking.
—— 1987: *A Thousand Plateaus*, trans. Brian Massumi. Minneapolis: University of Minnesota Press.
Derrida, Jacques 1992: Before the law. Trans. A. Ronell in D. Attridge (ed.), *Acts of Literature*, London: Routledge. (Originally presented at the 1982 Colloque de Cerisy on Lyotard.)
Dews, Peter 1987: *Logics of Disintegration*. London: Verso.
Ferry, Luc and Renaut, Alain 1985: *La Pensée 68*. Paris: Gallimard.

Frank, Manfred 1984: *Was ist Neostrukturalismus?* Frankfurt: Suhrkamp.
—— 1988a: Dissension et consensus selon Jean-François Lyotard et Jürgen Habermas. *Les Cahiers de Philosophie* (special issue on Lyotard), 5, 163–84.
—— 1988b: *Die Grenzen der Verständigung. Ein Geistesgespräch zwischen Lyotard und Habermas.* Frankfurt: Suhrkamp.
Freud, Sigmund 1971: *Beyond the Pleasure Principle*, trans. James Strachey. London: Hogarth Press.
Hegel, Georg Wilhelm Friedrich 1977: *Phenomenology of Spirit*, trans. A. V. Miller. Oxford: Clarendon Press.
Ingram, David 1992: The postmodern Kantianism of Arendt and Lyotard. In A. Benjamin (ed.), *Judging Lyotard*, London: Routledge.
Jameson, Fredric 1984: Foreword. In Lyotard 1984b, vii–xxii.
Kant Immanuel 1980: *The Critique of Judgement*, trans J. C. Meredith. Oxford: Clarendon Press.
—— 1990: The contest of faculties. In H. Reiss (ed.), *Kant's Political Writings*, Cambridge: Cambridge University Press.
Kripke, Saul 1980: *Naming and Necessity*. Oxford: Blackwell.
Lacoue-Labarthe, Philippe 1985: Où en étions nous? In Jacques Derrida (ed.), *La Faculté de juger*, Paris: Minuit.
Levinas, Emanuel 1969: *Totality and Infinity*, trans. A. Lingis. Dordrecht: Kluwer.
Lyotard, Jean-François 1948: Nés en 1925. *Temps Modernes*, 32, May, 2052–7.
—— 1954: *La Phénoménologie*. Paris: Presses Universitaires de France.
—— 1971: *Discours, figure*. Paris: Klincksieck.
—— 1973: *Dérive à partir de Marx et Freud*. Paris: Union Générale d'Éditions. (Trans. at 1984a.)
—— 1974: *Économie libidinale*. Paris: Minuit. (Trans. at 1993a.)
—— 1977: *Les Transformateurs Duchamp*. Paris: Galilée.
—— 1979a: *Au Juste*. Paris: Christian Bourgois. (Trans. at 1984b.)
—— 1979b: *La Condition postmoderne*. Paris: Minuit. (Trans. at 1985a.)
—— 1980a: *Des Dispositifs pulsionnels*, 2nd edn with new preface. Paris: Christian Bourgois. (First edn Paris: Union Générale d'Éditions, 1973.)
—— 1980b: *La Partie de peinture*. Cannes: Maryse Candela.
—— 1983: *Le Différend*. Paris: Minuit. (Trans. at 1988a.)
—— 1984a: *Driftworks*. New York: Semiotext(e).
—— 1984b: *The Postmodern Condition: a Report on Knowledge*, trans. Geoff Bennington and Brian Massumi. Manchester: Manchester University Press.
—— 1985a: *Just Gaming*, trans. Vlad Godzich. Minneapolis: University of Minnesota Press.
—— (ed.) 1985b: *Les Immatériaux*. Paris: Centre Georges Pompidou.
—— 1986: *L'Enthousiame: la critique kantienne de l'histoire*. Paris: Galilée.
—— 1988a: *The Differend: Phrases in Dispute*, trans. George Van Den Abeele. Manchester: Manchester University Press.
—— 1988b: *Heidegger et 'les juifs'*. Paris: Galilée.
—— 1988c: *L'Inhumain: causeries sur le temps*. Paris: Galilée. (Trans. at 1991.)
—— 1988d: *Peregrinations: Law, Form, Event*. New York: Columbia University Press. (This includes an excellent bibliography by Eddie Yeghiayan of works by and on Jean-François Lyotard.)
—— 1989a: *La Guerre des Algériens: Écrits, 1956–1963*, ed. M. Ramdani. Paris: Galilée. (Trans. at 1993c.)
—— 1989b: *The Lyotard Reader*, ed. A. Benjamin. Oxford: Blackwell.

Lyotard, Jean-François 1991: *The Inhuman: Reflections on Time*, trans. Geoffrey Bennington and Rachel Bowlby. Cambridge: Polity Press.

—— 1993a: *Libidinal Economy*, trans. Iain Hamilton Grant. London: Athlone.

—— 1993b: *Moralités postmodernes*. Paris: Galilée.

—— 1993c: *Political Writings*, trans. and ed. Bill Readings and Kevin Paul Geiman. London: UCL.

Nancy, Jean-Luc 1985: Dies irae. In Jacques Derrida (ed.), *La Faculté de juger*, Paris: Minuit.

—— 1991: Lapsus judicii. Trans. D. Webb and J. Williams. *Pli: The Warwick Journal of Philosophy*, 3.2, 16–40.

Norris, Christopher 1990: *What's Wrong with Postmodernism*. Hemel Hempstead: Harvester.

Raulet, Gérard 1984: From modernity as one-way street to postmodernity as dead-end. *New German Critique*, 33, Fall.

Readings, Bill 1991: *Introducing Lyotard: Art and Politics*. London: Routledge.

—— 1992: Pagans, perverts or primitives? Experimental justice in the empire of capital. In A. Benjamin (ed.), *Judging Lyotard*, London: Routledge.

—— 1993: Foreword: The end of the political. In Lyotard 1993.

Rogozinski, Jacob 1988: Argumenter avec Manfred Frank? *Les Cahiers de Philosophie* (special issue on Lyotard), 5, 185–92.

Rorty, Richard 1985: Le Cosmopolitanisme sans émancipation: en réponse à Jean-François Lyotard. Trans. P. Saint-Amand. *Critique*, no 41, May, 569–84. (Includes a discussion between Rorty and Lyotard.)

—— 1991: Habermas and Lyotard on postmodernity. In *Essays on Heidegger and Others*, Cambridge: Cambridge University Press.

Steuerman, Emilia 1992: Habermas vs Lyotard: modernity vs postmodernity. In A. Benjamin (ed.), *Judging Lyotard*, London: Routledge.

Wittgenstein, Ludwig 1953: *Philosophical Investigations*. Oxford: Blackwell.

Index